Norma Vally's

BATHROOM FIX-UPS

Bonus
DVD
Included

Norma Vally's

BATHROOM FIX-UPS

More Than 50 Projects for Every Skill Level

WILEY

Wiley Publishing, Inc.

Norma Vally's Bathroom Fix-ups

Published by Wiley Publishing, Inc., Hoboken, New Jersey

Library of Congress Cataloging-in-Publication Data:
Vally, Norma.
[Bathroom fix-ups]
Norma Vally's bathroom fix-ups : more than 50 projects for every skill level.
p. cm.
ISBN-13: 978-0-470-25156-0
ISBN-10: 0-470-25156-5
1. Bathrooms—Remodeling--Amateurs' manuals. 2. Bathrooms—Maintenance and repair—Amateurs' manuals. 3. Do-it-yourself work. 4. Women construction workers. I. Title. II. Title: Bathroom fix-ups.

TH4816.3.B37V35 2009
643'.52—dc22

2008046692

Printed in the United States of America

10 9 8 7 6 5 4 3 2 1

Book production by Wiley Publishing, Inc., Composition Services

credits

Acquisitions Editor
Pamela Mourouzis

Project Editor
Donna Wright

Editorial Manager
Christina Stambaugh

Publisher
Cindy Kitchel

Vice President and Executive Publisher
Kathy Nebenhaus

Interior Design
Tai Blanche

Project Photography
Matt Bowen

Illustrations
Ronda David-Burroughs
Karl Brandt
Brooke Graczyk
Shane Johnson

In dedication to my loving and inimitable Aunt Rose-Marie. Tender but tough, sweet and sour, extremely wise, unwittingly eccentric, ever giving, ever caring, ever funny, always there for me in more ways than I can count—everyone's favorite aunt—my deepest thanks for your constant love and support. I know you like things short and sweet, so I'll stop with the nya-nya, nya-nya, nya-nya. *You're the best. You're a star. I love you.*

acknowledgments

Writing these books reminds me of the proverb "It takes a village to raise a child." I've often referred to these books as my babies, and *raising* them certainly would not have been possible without the help of so many wonderful people. To the exceptional staff of Wiley Publishing, especially Cindy Kitchel, Pam Mourozis, and Donna Wright, and to Jason Marcuson and Jim Lightle at its onset—sincere thanks for your efforts and vision in creating this series. To my literary agent, Maura Teitelbaum, thank you for your continued support. For all of the technical assistance, tremendous thanks to Dave "The Heart" Carpenter, Bill "Stemmie" Harper (Big Daddy's Plumbing Repair Parts), Joe Barry (Ray Barry & Sons), Alfredo Anelli, and especially my cousin Sal Pino. Much thanks to Le Gourmet Kitchen—Bruce Colluci, Jonathan Salmon, and Jamie Gaudio (Silly Girl).

Huge appreciation to my beautiful family, especially Mama Grace, Brother Berto and Janne, Aunt Rose-Marie, and The Medinas. To all of my incredible friends, especially Lucia, Phyllis, Maria, Jordan, Aldo, JD, Barbara, and The Neils—thank you for putting up with my whining! Special thanks to Rick Medina for this series' inception and unceasing work and belief in me and our vision. Additional thanks to Eric McCullough, Michael Rhodes (The Home Depot), Ben Kunkel (Porter Paints), Cory Mennell (The Tile Shop), Eric Town (Fernco), Todd Kuhnert (Moen), Mitch Zoch (Eljer), Brasscraft, Neoperl, and especially the team at Ryobi.

Additional Photography

top left, p. 6: ©iStockphoto.com/Matjaz Boncina

top right, p. 6: ©iStockphoto.com/Tore Johannesen

bottom, p. 6: ©iStockphoto.com/FreezeFrameStudio

top, p. 7: ©iStockphoto.com/George Mayer

bottom, p. 7 and 186–187: ©iStockphoto.com/M. Eric Honeycutt

p. 12–23 and 140: ©iStockphoto.com/Terry J. Alcorn

p. 62–63: ©iStockphoto.com/Justin Horrocks

p. 122–123: ©iStockphoto.com/Dennis Guyitt

p. 135 and 151: ©iStockphoto.com/laughingmango

p. 145: ©iStockphoto.com/Howard Oates

a note from Norma

Paris, circa 1989, I'm on stage singing with a rock and roll band in the hottest night club at the time, *Les Bain Douches,* when Prince, that's right *Prince,* comes out on stage to do a song with the band. I nearly dropped dead.

How I got from that stage to swinging a hammer, TV shows, and books on home improvement? I have no idea . . . it would probably take years on a therapist's couch and a whole other book series to explain that one.

Here's what I do know, feeling helpless is never fun, especially in your own home. Something as simple as not knowing what to do as you watch your toilet bowl overflow onto the floor can be traumatizing. Without the know-how, means, or even opportunity of finding a qualified and trustworthy professional to manage a project will leave you feeling frustrated, exhausted . . . helpless.

When I started working construction in Brooklyn with my cousin Sal *umpteen* years ago, every job I walked in on, the initial reaction was always the same—they'd mumble behind my back, *What's she doing here?* They never thought I was a worker. *Is that his girlfriend? Is she here to take a coffee order? She must be the designer.* When I'd start hauling in sheetrock, strapping on a toolbelt, and getting to work heads turned, eyebrows raised, and the questions shifted to, "How did you learn how to do all this stuff?" My stock response, "Well it ain't brain surgery!"

Recognizing homeowners' feeling of helplessness motivated me to reach out and say to them, "Hey, if I can do this, so can you." I'm so grateful that I've been able to build various platforms that provide me with a means to get this message out there in an entertaining and empowering way.

I hope this book will give you the inspiration and information you need to make your bathroom the well-functioning and delightful spaces you want them to be.

I've often said, you can take the girl out of Brooklyn, but you can't take the Brooklyn out of the girl. So in closing, let me leave you with a Brooklyn-spirited motto that I've come up with—words I think we can all live by—Go Fix, YOURSELF!

Thank you!

Live happy,

Norma Vally

Introduction

In the neighborhood where I live when I'm in Brooklyn (and where I used to live in France), it's commonplace to shop at a specific store for a particular product. You go to the bakery for bread, the fish market for clams, the butcher for lamb shank, the candy shop for jelly rings, and so on. While it's not the quick one-stop-shop you get from supermarkets or club stores, it's the only real way to get that authentic, freshly prepared, hard-to-find, imported or domestic, mouthwatering good stuff. You can feel it the moment you walk into that particular shop, take a sniff, and know exactly why you're in there—oh, the semolina bread just came out of the oven. I'll take four loaves, please!

In this book I sought to bring that specialty shop intensity to the reader. It's jampacked with detailed projects and topics as they relate to a particular part of your home. I believe that total submersion is the most powerful way to excite, educate, and enrich a do-it-yourselfer. Blanket topic books certainly have their place, as do the mega-marts of America, but when you want to get into the nitty-gritty, down and dirty of a particular space in your home, this is the book to dive into.

About This Book

It's as easy as one-two-three! Yeah, right. I actually resent how loosely the expression is used, especially when it comes to home improvement. In my book, you won't find "tah-dah" and the perfectly formed cake pops out of the oven, or in this case, the shiny new faucet on the sink deck. Granted, some projects are easier than others, but often obstacles come up in the simplest of projects, making one-two-three more like one through sixty-four. I paid careful attention to inform the reader about all the pertinent scenarios that may arise when working on a particular project, even what you should consider before getting started.

I enjoy conveying information in a way that's fun, clear, and approachable. Be it through labeled illustrations or shooting-from-the-hip straight talk, I animate the projects so the reader can be comfortable with them. Even more, I literally bring projects to life with the enclosed DVD that highlights particular how-to's—I'm doing them, right there in front of you, step by step. These projects are identified with a DVD icon in the book.

How This Book Is Organized

This book is organized into four parts. The first three parts address projects that increase in degree of difficulty—simple to moderate to advanced—with the last part stepping outside how-to and into design. Each project includes a "Consider This" section. I provide these points so you can fully wrap your brain around pertinent aspects of each project—from drying times to potential complications and warnings. Before getting started on the core project, I present a "Prep Work" section. Prep work is sometimes the most important part of a project so you can better plan how to tackle it.

While compiling projects for this book, it struck me that home improvement projects remind me of treatments on a spa menu. A telltale sign of a spa junkie, I'll admit, but isn't it true that "makeovers" relate to homes as well as to people? So I ask, do you want a quick rejuvenating makeover or an intensive overhaul? Is it simply the grout that needs refreshing or do you need to retile the tub surround? Hence, these chapters are broken down as though they were selections from a spa menu, where in this case, your home gets the treatment and you, my dear reader, are the cosmetologist.

■ PART 1: EXPRESS FACELIFT

This section offers quick, easy, and inexpensive projects. If you don't have the time, skill level, or budget, you can still make refreshing fixes to your bathroom that will improve your overall bath-time experience. A beginner will thrive in this section.

The little wiggle of your loose towel bar, the spots of mold in your grout, the slow-draining sink—while individually each of these is small stuff, together they add up to a big pain in the butt (no potty pun intended). Little by little, the small stuff robs us of the bathroom bliss we should all know and love. In fact, you may literally break into a sweat when that clogged toilet overflows all over the bathroom floor.

We go after the small stuff in this section and quickly knock these little fixes off our to-do list to reclaim our lavatory love with ease and minimal expense.

■ PART 2: CORRECTIVE TREATMENT

This section tackles projects that go deeper than the surface. Here, you're repairing at a level that requires small investments of time and money but gives a big impact. If you consider yourself "kind of handy," these projects will be a breeze.

Big bang for your buck describes the type of projects covered in this section. Say hello to your new handheld shower! Say goodbye to that running toilet! And now you can install that over the toilet cabinet you've always wanted—finally a place to keep all your skin- and hair-care products.

■ PART 3: INTENSIVE TREATMENT

This section tackles larger, more complex tasks. Although we're not tearing out rooms and changing footprints, we are going after projects that require a more advanced skill level than a novice do-it-yourselfer might have. I'm very excited about this section because we can really roll up our sleeves and dig into meaty projects. The complexity of them requires and assumes a working knowledge of all basic construction aspects: plumbing, electric, carpentry, and masonry.

Know that, while I've tried to account for many of the different scenarios and challenges that may accompany a project (so you're not left in the lurch saying "Hey, wait a minute . . . that's not in the book!"), it's impossible to predict and cover them all. Let me say, through experience, *expect* to hit roadblocks here and there; they just come with the home-improvement territory.

I always encourage DIYers to step out of their comfort zone and tackle bigger and bigger projects but not without first being fully aware of the safety aspects and ramifications that accompany them. Read through the entire project first, paying careful attention to all the points within the "Consider This" section. Then get out there and have yourself a fixin' good time!

■ PART 4: TOTAL INDULGENCE: DREAMING UP THE PERFECT BATHROOM

Using this section, you can knock down all barriers of entry for you to be able to dream up your perfect bathroom. Speaking of knocking down, I'll explore changing the layout, or even the footprint, of your bathroom—projects typically best left to remodeling professionals. I'll guide you into what's best for you and your family's bathroom needs.

When you read this section, put the do-it-yourself aspect and budget aside. Let the sky be the limit! Fully indulge your senses and discover all the innovative and exciting materials, trends, and designs that are available for bathrooms today. I encourage dreaming big and exploring all options so when you take those first steps to professionally remodeling your bathroom, you'll know what *going big* can really mean.

Mama always told me to reach for the stars—the worst thing that can happen is you'll land on the moon . . . or a remote-controlled toilet, in this case.

Part 1

Express Facelift

Sinks

Low water pressure? A faucet that jiggles? A dull sink finish? Give your sink all of the rejuvenating little repairs it so desperately needs.

Clean a Pop-up

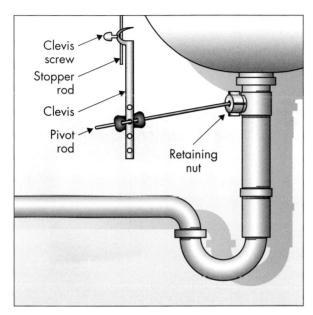

Clevis
screw

Stopper
rod

Clevis

Pivot
rod

Retaining
nut

Very often, all that stands between you and a well-draining sink is a clump of hair tangled around the bottom of your pop-up. It's hard to believe how much hair ends up accumulating there if you don't actually wash your hair in the sink, but trust me, it finds its way down the drain. Whether you're brushing your hair over the sink or rinsing your hands of hair gel, over time, hair strands build up and obstruct water from passing through the pipe.

The hair clog may also inhibit the pop-up from closing properly when you try to fill the sink with water—water slowly drains down because the hair prevents the stopper from creating a tight seal. For this reason, it's a good idea to clean your pop-up regularly to prevent slow drainage.

WHAT YOU'LL NEED

Tongue-and-groove pliers
Garbage bag
Flashlight**
Old pillow or blanket**
Gloves**

** Optional

CONSIDER THIS

Some pop-ups don't require any disassembly and can be pulled out from the top of the sink. If this is the type you have, simply pull out the pop-up and clean off the hair clog. Remember to have a garbage bag handy to discard the hair and muck. (Be prepared—it ain't pretty.)

PREP WORK

- Working under a sink is always cramped and awkward. To make more room for yourself, remove all your under-the-sink articles. (How do we accumulate so much stuff?)

- Put down an old pillow or blanket to lie on so that you can be more comfortable as you're working.

- Stand a lit flashlight inside the vanity for better visibility.

THE PROJECT

1 Locate the retaining nut under the sink.

2 With pliers, unscrew the retaining nut and pull it back onto the pivot rod. Do not run the water after you've loosened the retaining nut of the pop-up; it will leak from that opening.

3 Pull back the pivot rod until the pivot ball is visible; this will release the stopper.

4 Pull out the stopper from the top of the sink and clean off the hair and muck.

5 Reinsert the clean stopper and push the pivot rod back into its original position. You'll need to catch the hole at the bottom of the stopper with the tip of the pivot rod, which can be a little tricky. Slowly twist the stopper until the hole lines up with the pivot rod. You'll know you've got it when you tug on the stopper and it doesn't come out.

6 Tighten the retaining nut with the pliers.

7 To be sure the pop-up is screwed in properly, close the pop-up, fill the sink with water, release the pop-up, and see if water drips from the retaining nut. If it does, snug down the retaining nut a bit more.

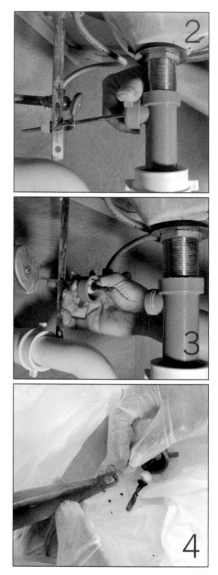

Do you smell foul odors from your drain?

Have you ever noticed that when you first run water, a nasty odor wafts up from the drain? What you're smelling comes from a residue that builds up along the pipe between the drain and the *P-trap* (the U-shaped curve of pipe under the sink). The P-trap holds water that acts as a barrier to prevent sewer gases from backing up into the drain, yet, it can't stop odors from a "bio-film" that grows along the pipe between the P-trap and the sink. To remove this bio-film, simply remove the stopper or strainer and scrub with a disinfectant cleanser. Then scrub down the drain pipe with a bottle brush.

Faucet Aerator Maintenance

WHAT YOU'LL NEED

Tongue-and-groove pliers
Masking tape
Old toothbrush
Penetrating oil*

* If applicable

Is the flow at your faucet down to a drizzle? It's probably a clogged aerator. The *aerator* is a small filtering device at the tip of your faucet. It contains a screen (or screens) that serves two functions— filtering out particles and creating a smooth, consistent flow of water.

Over time, the screen can get clogged and cause a reduction in water pressure as it flows out of the faucet. These particles may also cause the spout to sputter. Simply cleaning the screen will get that full flow going again.

CONSIDER THIS

Whenever you take something apart, be sure to remember what order the pieces go in. In this instance, place the aerator parts down one at a time and in order from left to right, as if you're creating an "exploded" view of the aerator and all its parts. Then work from the reverse when putting it back together.

PREP WORK

- Close the drain so that you don't lose any parts of the aerator.
- If the faucet is old or you can see built-up mineral deposits around the aerator, spray the aerator with penetrating oil and let it soak in for about 15 minutes to make the unscrewing easier.
- Wrap the plier jaws with masking tape to prevent damage to the faucet.

THE PROJECT

1 With the pliers, unscrew the aerator.

2 Brush out the screen. Depending on the aerator, there may be more than one screen with accompanying rings. Carefully pull them apart and brush out the particles. Also brush out any buildup around the outside of the aerator. Soaking it in vinegar may help, but do not let it sit for too long as the vinegar could mar the finish.

3 Run the water without the aerator in place to flush out mineral deposits—you may be surprised at what comes out. (See how the water goes chug-a-lug without the aerator in place?)

4 Reassemble the aerator and screw it back to the faucet. Snug it tight with the pliers.

Restricted-Flow Washing Machine

This same type of aerator clog happens to your washer. If you notice that the water is flowing into your washer with very low pressure, follow the preceding steps, with a few modifications: First, shut off the water to the washer from the shut-off valves. Unscrew the hoses and brush out the screens—you'll be amazed at how much debris has built-up from your water!

Tighten a Loose Faucet

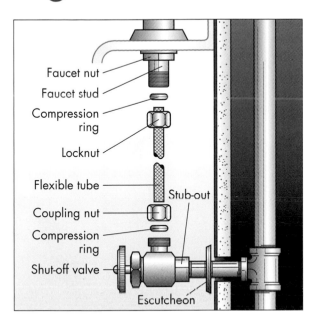

Faucet nut
Faucet stud
Compression ring
Locknut
Flexible tube
Coupling nut
Compression ring
Shut-off valve
Stub-out
Escutcheon

If your faucet is sliding around the top of the sink, here's the fix for you. The nuts of the faucet under the sink have loosened and are no longer securing the faucet snugly to the sink.

CONSIDER THIS

To prevent your faucet from loosening in the future, it's important not to jar or tug on the handles or spout—as when kids use the spout like a grab handle to hoist themselves up high enough to reach the sink. Aggressive wear and tear may lead to a more serious problem that won't be an easy fix.

WHAT YOU'LL NEED

Basin wrench or tongue-and-groove pliers

Rubber washers*

Penetrating oil*

Flashlight**

Old pillow or blanket**

* If applicable

** Optional

PREP WORK

- Working under a sink is always cramped and awkward. To make more room for yourself, remove all your under-the-sink articles.

- Put down an old pillow or blanket to lie on so that you can be more comfortable as you're working.

- Stand a lit flashlight inside the vanity for better visibility.

- If the nuts seem corroded and unmovable, spray them with penetrating oil and let them soak.

THE PROJECT

1 Examine the locknuts under your faucet and try to tighten them by hand.

2 If hand-tightening doesn't work, use your pliers or basin wrench to tighten the nuts under the faucet until they're snug. Do not force a plastic nut because you might crack it!

3 If the nuts have bottomed out, add a couple of rubber washers to the nut—this will add more depth to allow the nut to grab against the sink and pull down the faucet. To do so, first shut off the water at the shut-off valves, unscrew the supply lines with tongue-and-groove pliers, and then unscrew the nuts. Now you can add a couple of rubber washers inside the nuts.

4 Screw everything back into place, being careful not to over-tighten a plastic nut.

Basin Wrench

A *basin wrench* is a specialized plumbing tool that I highly recommend owning. It makes easy work of loosening and tightening fittings when there is limited space or access to reach a nut or hose coupling underneath a basin or lavatory. Without one, something as simple as loosening a faucet nut can be next to impossible to accomplish—certainly not without a lot of cursing and sweating!

Resurface a Sink Finish

WHAT YOU'LL NEED

Most refinishing kits include several of the items listed below. After choosing your paint or kit, see which items you still need from this list.

Screwdriver

Razor scraper

Plastic scraper

Eye protection

Organic vapor mask

Fan (if there is no window)

Nonlatex gloves

Sponge, rag, and bucket

Sink cleanser (like Ajax)

Porcelain etching solution

220-grit wet/dry sandpaper

Masking tape

Tack cloth

Two-part epoxy paint

Stir stick

Roller tray

4 high-density foam rollers and 1 roller handle (4 inches)

2-inch polyester brush

Plastic bags

Lacquer thinner

Caulk

Caulking gun

Polyester putty (like Bondo; also called filler)

Alkyd-based primer for metal*

* If applicable

Is your sink old and dingy looking? Do you scrub and scrub, but it still seems dirty? If you're ready for a fresh-looking sink, but you aren't ready for the work or cost involved in installing a new one, this project is for you!

Sinks and tubs are actually resurfaced (or *reglazed*) with epoxy paint. Epoxy is most commonly known as a high-performance adhesive. In this application, epoxy adds an extremely durable adhesive property to paint, making it ideal for resurfacing sinks, tubs, and even tiles.

In the past, I would only have recommended that you hire a professional to refinish a sink or tub, but today there are kits on the market for DIYers that are user-friendly and nontoxic.

While I don't recommend resurfacing a kitchen sink or a tub that gets a lot of wear and tear, a bathroom sink gets just the right amount and type of use to keep the finish looking new. Just be sure not to pour nail polish remover down the sink, as it may cause the finish to blister.

CONSIDER THIS

This resurfacing project relates to porcelain and ceramic sinks. Be sure that the product you choose works on your sink's surface.

The resurfacing process is very time sensitive. The area must be allowed to dry for 24 hours before you paint. You'll need to wait several hours between coats. Most products don't cure completely for several days. This means that the sink must be off-limits during this time. Another time issue is work time—rollers can't sit for extended periods, and once paint parts are mixed together, the paint sometimes has to stand for close to an hour before it can be used.

Resurfacing products are temperature and humidity sensitive. Generally, they cannot be used at under 65°F or over 80 percent humidity.

Epoxy paints can be tinted to match your fixtures. Follow the manufacturer's tinting instructions. Otherwise, basic white and almond are readily available.

Use only an epoxy paint that is nontoxic and lead free when completely dry.

The products used in this project give off strong fumes, so be prepared to work in a ventilated environment; open a window or bring in a fan if necessary. Above all, strictly follow all the manufacturer's directions and safety precautions.

PREP WORK

Especially with this project, great results rely completely on thorough prep work. You must follow all steps stringently. Don't try to skip or rush through any steps—you'll end up with a poor finish. So have patience!

- Remove all caulking (see the Prep Work section on page 35 in Chapter 3).

- Remove detachable faucet parts (like handles and the stopper). If any exposed metal is worn, coat it with an alkyd primer to protect the finish. (Follow the manufacturer's instructions.) This product must dry completely before you continue.

- Sand any rust spots and scrape away any loose particles.

- Fill any cracks or chips with polyester filler. (Follow the manufacturer's instructions.) This product must dry completely before you continue.

- Wash down the entire surface with cleanser. Rinse thoroughly with water.

- Apply the porcelain etching solution. (Follow the manufacturer's instructions.) Rinse thoroughly with water, twice.

- Sand the sink surface with wet/dry sandpaper. Be sure to keep wetting the sandpaper as you work around the surface (a).

- Rinse completely until no grit is left. From this point forward, do not touch the sink surface with your bare hands—the oils from your skin will impede proper adhesion of the paint.

- Let the entire area dry for at least 24 hours.

- Tape off the edges, the drain, and the faucet with masking tape.

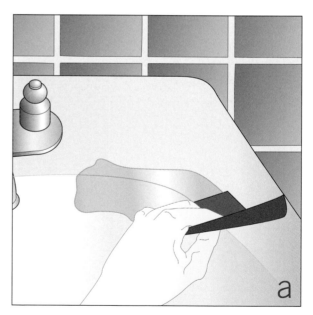

THE PROJECT

1 Wipe down the surface with tack cloth. Remove all the dust and lint—it's crucial to work in a dust-free environment.

2 Mix together the epoxy paint parts. (Follow the manufacturer's instructions.)

3 Pour about one-third of the mixed epoxy paint into the roller tray. Evenly coat the roller and begin rolling the sink.

4 Coat the entire surface with a thin layer of paint. Paint slowly and gently. To avoid runs, do not overload the roller with paint. Use the brush to get to areas the roller can't reach. Don't try to roll over areas that have begun to dry. It's normal if some of the original surface shows through the first coat.

5 Let dry according to the manufacturer's instructions, and then repeat with a second coat. Start with a fresh roller. You may need to apply a third coat.

6 Allow the sink to dry and cure as indicated. Keep the sink off-limits and dust free during this time.

7 Reapply caulking if needed.

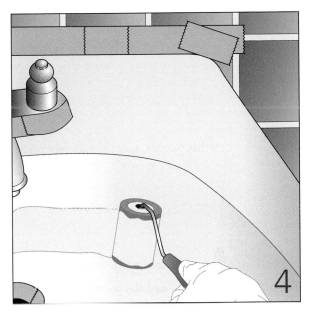

Refinishing Plastic and Fiberglass Surfaces

You can refresh plastic and fiberglass sinks and tub surrounds with a refinishing kit designed especially for these surfaces. This product is typically a water-based formula, which means that it's easier to work with—it has shorter drying times and less fumes, and it cleans up with soap and water.

Showers

Is it asking too much to have a shower that properly drains and a showerhead that doesn't drip? Certainly not! Check out how the simple projects in this chapter can revive your shower.

Clean a Shower Stall Drain

WHAT YOU'LL NEED

Flathead and Phillips screwdrivers
Needle-nose pliers
Cutting pliers
Waterproof gloves
Wire hanger
Plastic bag

There are few things I hate more than when I'm showering and dirty water starts backing up out of the drain and accumulating around my ankles. Gross! The culprit is undoubtedly a hair/soap-scum clog. Instead of using harsh chemicals to clean out a slow drain, it's easier and safer to pull the clog out from the drain hole.

CONSIDER THIS

Be forewarned: What you pull up from this clog will be slimy and super-yucky. Know that your bravery will be rewarded! It's well worth the gross factor when you see that your shower water drains away effortlessly.

PREP WORK

- Unscrew the strainer grate. Once it's unscrewed, a flathead screwdriver may help you pry it out. Your type of strainer may just pop out (a). In that case, use needle-nose pliers or a flathead screwdriver to help pull it out. Work gently so that you don't bend or crack the strainer.

- Set the strainer and screws aside; be careful not to let those little screws fall down the drain.

- Cut the wire hanger and bend it into a straight length. On one end, with the pliers, bend a ¾-inch hook.

THE PROJECT

1 Fish the wire hanger down the drain far enough until you hit something.

2 Twist around the wire hanger and try to catch the hook onto part of the clog.

3 When you feel you've grabbed something, slowly pull up the wire.

4 Remove the wad from the hook and go back for more.

5 When you feel the entire clog is out, flush with hot water.

Clean a Showerhead

WHAT YOU'LL NEED

Plastic food-storage bag (large enough to fit over the showerhead)

Heavy-duty tape

White vinegar

Old toothbrush

Large needle or pin

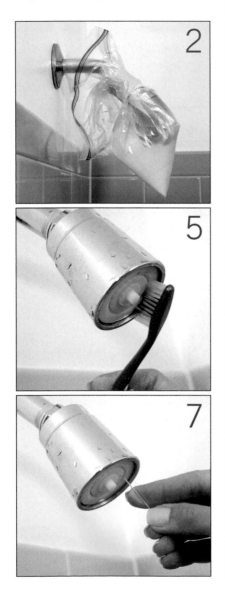

Over time, mineral deposits from water will clog your showerhead, turning an exhilarating shower into a dull drizzle. Good luck trying to rinse out shampoo. All that white chalky stuff can easily be removed with a few common household articles.

CONSIDER THIS

This project uses a vinegar soaking solution to dissolve mineral deposits, which will improve the water pressure. Some fixture finishes may be damaged by overexposure to vinegar or any mineral deposit cleanser, especially if they are already old and worn. To avoid damaging the finish, check the manufacturer's warranty. I also recommend checking the showerhead frequently while it's soaking to see if any signs of pitting begin.

Allow up to several hours of showerhead soaking, which means that this shower will be unavailable until you've completed this project.

THE PROJECT

1. Fill the plastic bag approximately ⅓ full with vinegar (enough to submerge the face of the showerhead).

2. Squeeze the bag closed around the shower arm and seal it closed with tape.

3. Let it soak for up to several hours.

4. Remove the plastic bag, being careful not to splash vinegar in your eyes.

5. Scrub the showerhead face with the toothbrush.

6. Let the water run through the showerhead for several seconds.

7. If you see some outlet holes that are still clogged, use the needle or pin to poke them open.

8. Run water through the showerhead again and repeat the hole-poking if necessary.

Replace a Standard Shower Rod with a Curved Rod

WHAT YOU'LL NEED

I strongly recommend purchasing an adjustable shower rod because it'll save you from having to measure or cut the rod—plus it accommodates tubs from approximately 4½ to 6 feet in length. Most shower-rod kits include many of the following materials. Check the package for materials included, and then see which items you still need from this list.

Adjustable curved shower-rod kit

Flathead and Phillips screwdrivers

Drill/driver

Masonry or drywall drill bit (see kit instructions for size)

Rubber mallet

Pencil

Masking tape

Tape measure

Level

Wall anchors

Screws

I'm always so grossed out by shower curtains that stick to me as I'm trying to soap down and rinse. What's worse is when the curtain or liner is less than new—shall we say *mildewy.* I feel like I have to shower after my shower.

Happily, today there are new crescent-shaped rods that increase shower space by 25 percent. Also, because the mounts are curved, wrapping in toward the tub, less water splashes out, making a curved rod not only more comfortable but functional.

CONSIDER THIS

Straight shower-rod mounting brackets will not fit a new curved rod because the placement will shift farther in toward the tub due to the curve. This means you'll have to patch the old screw holes. Whether your old shower rod is mounted on drywall or in tile will determine what kind of patch you will need to make. For step-by-step instructions on how to make drywall repairs, see page 52 in Chapter 5. For replacing tile, see the project on page 31 in this chapter.

I suggest allowing the drywall patch or tile to dry for several hours before installing the new shower rod. This way, you'll avoid accidentally hitting the patch or tile and damaging it before it's had a chance to harden.

Always follow the manufacturer's directions, but the following steps will give you a thorough guide on how to replace any bracket-mounted shower rod.

PREP WORK

- Remove the old shower rod. If it's mounted with brackets (not a tension rod), locate the screws, unscrew them, and remove the rod. If the screws are not visible, you'll need to lift the decorative cover off the bracket to reveal the screws.

- Patch the old screw holes as dictated by your wall type.

THE PROJECT

1 Determine the desired shower-rod height by measuring the length of your shower curtain. Measure up from the floor and mark the height on both sides. Also, measure how deep you want the shower-rod placement, and mark that same distance on both sides.

2 With a pencil, mark the holes of the bracket on the wall. Tape the enclosed template (if supplied) on the wall to mark the hole placement.

3 With the appropriate drill bit, drill your holes. If you hit a wood stud, stop drilling as soon as you're past the wall.

4 Tap in anchors—use the rubber mallet if necessary. If you drilled into a stud, no anchors are necessary.

5 Screw in one template with the rod attached. Slip the decorative bracket caps (if supplied) over the rod at this time, facing them in the right orientation to cover each bracket.

6 Attach the rod into the second bracket, and then secure the bracket on the opposite side with one screw. Check for level. If you messed up your hole placement, now is the time to fix it, which could mean redrilling the holes.

7 When you're sure the rod is level, secure all the screws in the bracket.

8 Slip the decorative caps over the brackets and you're done!

Which bit has the right bite?

Choosing the right bit for the right job is imperative. Not only must the size be right, but the *type* has to be right as well. The right type depends on the material you're drilling into and the type of hole you want to make. Another factor to consider is what the bit is made of. Generally, the more expensive the bit, the longer it will stay sharp. The bit world is vast, but the ones I've listed here (from left to right) will get you through most home-improvement projects.

Twist bits are the most common bits and are used to make small holes in various materials. *Masonry bits* are used for drilling in concrete, tile, stone, and so on. *Hole-saw bits* bore out a solid core through many materials. *Paddle* or *spade bits* pierce a center point and cut quickly through wood by scraping material away. *Countersink bits* make a dimple in material to allow the head of a screw to sit flush to a surface. I prefer to use a *pilot-bit/countersink* combination because you get your pilot hole and countersink all in one shot.

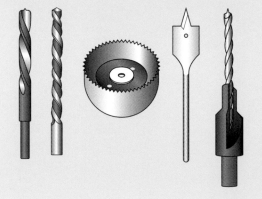

Fix a Leaky Showerhead

WHAT YOU'LL NEED

12-inch tongue-and-groove pliers

Pipe wrench*

Penetrating oil

Masking tape

Replacement O-ring or washer

Rag

Teflon tape or pipe putty

* If applicable

When your showerhead is leaking from its connection to the shower arm, the fix is as easy as a new washer and couple of spins of Teflon tape.

CONSIDER THIS

It is very important not to force the showerhead loose. Doing so could crack or strip the showerhead nut. Even worse, forcing could cause you to loosen the shower arm from the pipe behind the wall. If the head seems stuck, spray down the nut with penetrating oil and let it soak for a while.

Along the same line, do not over-tighten the showerhead. Over-tightening could crack the fitting or compress the washer to a point that it will no longer hold a seal.

PREP WORK

- Spray down the showerhead fitting with penetrating oil.
- Wrap the pliers and wrench jaws with masking tape to avoid scratching the metal on the showerhead.

THE PROJECT

1 Unscrew the showerhead, turning the pliers counterclockwise.

2 If it's really stuck, use a pipe wrench to hold back on the shower arm. Gripping firmly on the shower arm with this wrench will keep it stationary as you unscrew the head from the arm with the pliers. Sometimes it's easier to do this with a second person holding the wrench and you unscrewing with the pliers.

3 Remove the O ring washer (or rubber washer as seen in the photo) from the showerhead and use it to match with a replacement washer.

4 Clean out any old washer debris from the head and insert the new washer.

5 With a rag, remove any old Teflon tape or pipe putty from the threads of the shower arm.

6 Wrap the Teflon tape clockwise around the shower arm threads, no more than two to three spins—more isn't better here.

7 Screw the showerhead back onto the arm—first by hand, and then snug it with the pliers.

8 Turn on the water and check for leaks. If you see a leak, snug it some more, being careful not to over-tighten.

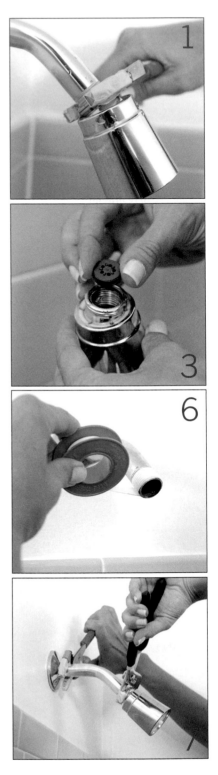

Secure or Replace a Loose or Cracked Tile

WHAT YOU'LL NEED

Replacement tiles*

Nail set and hammer*

Drill/driver*

¼-inch masonry drill bit*

Small pry bar or putty knife

Grout saw

Masonry "cold" chisel or dull wood chisel*

Scraper

Notched trowel*

Grout tile float

Matching premixed or powdered grout

Mixing pail and stir stick (for powdered grout)*

Safety glasses

Gloves

Large towel or tarp

Rags

Tile adhesive

Tile spacer (sized according to your grout line)

Large man-made tile sponge

Bucket of water

* If applicable

A loose tile in a shower stall or tub enclosure should be fixed as soon as possible. If a tile is moving, water can get behind it and damage the wall underneath. This trapped moisture will instigate mold growth and eventually cause more tiles to loosen and fall out completely.

CONSIDER THIS

The wall behind the tile you're fixing must be dry before you re-glue the tile. You can use a hair dryer on the wall to speed up the drying time.

You must allow 24 hours of drying time between gluing and grouting the tile before it can get wet or be disturbed. In other words, that shower stall or tub should be off-limits for 2 days.

You run the risk of breaking the tile when you're prying it out. Know that you may need to have a replacement tile on hand.

Be careful! Tile shards are very sharp. Wear safety gloves and glasses.

PREP WORK

- Plug the drain with a rag and cover the basin with a towel or tarp.

- You will want to reuse the tile, so work gently to remove it in one piece. Be mindful not to disturb the surrounding tiles.

- If it's very loose, it will be easy to pry out with a small pry bar or putty knife. Firmly but carefully insert the tip of the pry bar or knife into the loose section of the joint, and then slowly pry the tile away from the wall.

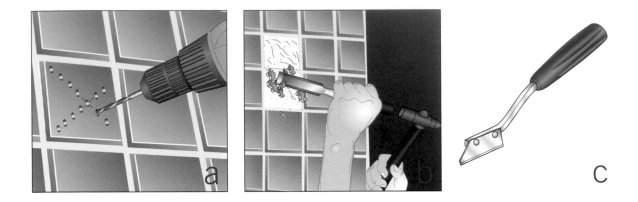

- If the tile is stubborn, you'll need to break it out. First, scrape out the old grout joints. Then punch small divots in a big X across the face of the tile with the nail set and hammer. With the divots as starting points, drill holes through the tile *(but not the wall)* to weaken it and create a break point (a). Now break out the tile in small pieces with the hammer and chisel (b).

- Once the tile is out, scrape off the adhesive from the wall with the scraper.

- Use a grout saw (c) to clean the edges of the adjoining tiles on the wall. Small bits of adhesive may remain—as long as no big bumps are left, it will be fine.

- Use the scraper to remove adhesive from the tile.

- If the wall is damp from water that has seeped behind the tile, allow it to dry completely before continuing.

Drilling Tips for Tile

When drilling into tile, there are a couple of special tidbits you should know about. First, only use an appropriate-sized masonry bit. Carbide tips are great for ceramic, but for porcelain, which is more dense, diamond tips work best.

Second, know that the bit will want to "walk" on you—the bit will spin off the drill point center as you're trying to drive the bit. You can prevent the bit from walking by making a divot in the tile surface with a nail set and hammer—an etched starting point that the bit can bite into. Just be careful not to hammer too hard and crack the tile (unless you're breaking the tile out).

Another trick is to put duct tape right over the spot you need to drill—the tape creates enough traction for the bit to dig in. Just transfer the drill spot to the tape so you know where it is.

Last, start drilling slowly, at a low speed, and with steady, firm pressure. Too much pressure will break the tile; too little won't penetrate. It's a delicate dance that takes some practice.

THE PROJECT

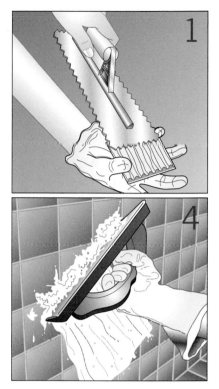

1 When you're sure that the wall is dry and particle free, spread the tile adhesive on the back of the tile using the short end of the trowel or scraper. Run grooves through the glue. Do the same to the wall space.

2 Insert the tile in the space and gently press it into place by taping it with the butt of your fist. Check that the tile is sitting flush with the others. Wipe away any glue that may have squeezed out to the surface.

3 Stick the tile spacers in between the grout lines and allow it to dry overnight.

4 To fill in the grout lines, use a grout float to press the grout into the joints of the tile lines. It's best to hold the float at an angle and pass over the area firmly in a diagonal direction.

5 With a damp sponge, gently wipe away the grout that remains on the face of the tile.

6 As the grout dries, a powdery residue will form. Gently wipe it away with a soft, clean rag, being careful not to wipe out any of the grout.

Bathtubs

When did tub-time stop being fun-time? Are moldy caulking, dingy tile, and stained grout cramping your style? Find out how to toss out these killjoys with projects from this chapter.

Re-Caulk a Tub or Faucet

WHAT YOU'LL NEED

Razor scraper

Utility knife

Disinfectant cleaner

Rag or paper towels

Bathroom caulking

Caulking gun

Baby oil

Caulk remover product**

Wire hanger*

* If applicable

** Optional

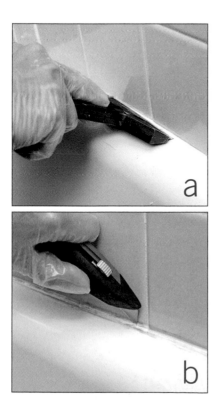

An improper seal on your tub and faucet is not only unsightly, but can allow water to seep behind your fixtures and tile, damaging the wall, decreasing tile stability, and creating a breeding ground for mold!

CONSIDER THIS

Caulking should not be touched or get wet before it's totally dry, so be sure to read the manufacturer's suggested drying time. My experience is that it's best to let it dry for at least 24 hours.

Caulking should never be applied to a wet or even damp surface—it will never adhere properly. If the area around your faucet or sink is waterlogged, allow it to dry out. You can use a blow dryer to speed up the drying time.

While several different caulking varieties exist, they can basically be broken down into two types—latex based and silicone based. Latex-based caulking is water soluble, so it can be cleaned up with water. Silicone-based caulking cannot be cleaned up with water, making it more difficult to work with. The upside of silicone is that it's extremely durable. Whichever you choose, be sure to buy one that indicates it is waterproof and mildew resistant.

PREP WORK

- Using the razor scraper, carefully scrape away the old caulking. Hold the scraper at an angle so as not to damage the tub or faucet surface (a). Score the caulk with a utility knife to break the seal if the caulk is difficult to remove (b).

- Make sure to scrape away all caulk and mineral-deposit residue.

- If there is considerable caulk residue that you're having trouble removing with the razor scraper, try a caulk-remover product. Wipe it on and let it soak in according to the manufacturer's directions. (**Note:** If the old caulking is silicone based, this product won't work. I recommend good, old elbow grease because the chemicals needed to break down silicone are highly toxic and nasty.)

- Wash the entire area with a disinfectant cleaner and let it dry thoroughly.

• Fill the tub with water and work in the tub barefooted so that the weight pulls the tub down and fully opens the joint. Just don't splash around as you work.

THE PROJECT

1 Cut open the caulking tube at an angle, and pierce the seal inside the nozzle with the caulking gun's provided piercer or the tip of a wire hanger if your gun doesn't come with one.

2 Load the gun and push forward on the plunger of the gun until it hits the back of the tube.

3 Put the nozzle of the gun on one side of the sink or faucet and begin squeezing the trigger.

4 As the caulk flows out, drag the tip of the gun along the edge of the sink or faucet. Do this until one side has a continuous bead of caulking.

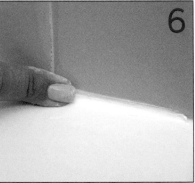

5 Release the plunger (so it doesn't continue to push out caulking) and put the gun down.

6 Wet the tip of your finger with a few drops of baby oil. Run your finger gently over the caulking, smoothing out the bead.

7 As excess caulking accumulates on your finger, wipe it on a rag or paper towel and continue along the bead.

8 Repeat Steps 3–7 until all sides are complete, and then let the caulking dry thoroughly.

Caulking Here, There, and Everywhere!

The steps from this project can also be used to re-caulk around the sink and shower stall. Exterior doors and windows can be sealed with exterior-grade caulking as well. Painter's caulking is perfect for a finished look around molding. Just be sure to use the appropriate caulking for the job at hand. For example, most silicone-based caulking cannot be painted. That means if you are planning on painting it to match, say, the molding color of your door, the paint would just bead away—yikes! So be sure to read the labels.

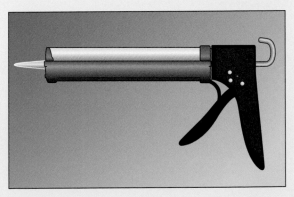

Unclog a Tub

WHAT YOU'LL NEED

Flathead and Phillips screwdrivers

Rubber gloves

Eye protection (if drain cleaner has been used)*

Heatproof plumber's grease

Old toothbrush or small wire brush

Rags

Plunger

Petroleum jelly

Baking soda

White vinegar

Boiling water

*If applicable

Some of us who have tried to clean out the tub drain were stopped dead in our tracks at Step 1—"How can I clean out the drain if I can't pull out the pop-up?" What makes it so daunting is that all the "guts" are hidden behind the tub walls—unlike a sink, where you can peek under the vanity to see what's going on. In this project, you get an inside look at your bathtub and how to get it draining like a dream.

If you're lucky enough to have a tub stopper that simply pulls out, skip the Prep Work section and go to the steps where the pop-up and trip lever are already removed.

CONSIDER THIS

Be warned! If you have already poured a chemical drain cleaner down your tub drain, but the clog still persists, proceed with extreme caution. Wear rubber gloves and eye protection, and work with the fan on or a window open. These drain cleaners are very toxic, so take all of these precautions seriously. You do not want to be unprotected if any of the drain cleaner (or even its fumes) comes splashing up as you're trying to pull out the stopper assembly.

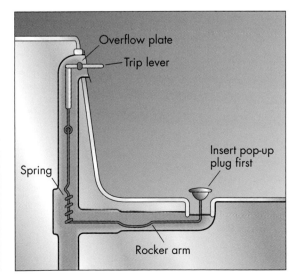

Overflow plate

Trip lever

Insert pop-up plug first

Spring

Rocker arm

PREP WORK

- Put the trip lever in the full open position and wiggle out the stopper and rocker arm. This may take some patience. If you have a plunge-type stopper, there's no visible stopper to pull out. In this case, simply unscrew the strainer.

- Unscrew the trip-lever plate (be careful not to drop the screws down the drain).

- Pull out the entire trip-lever assembly (a).

- Remove any debris from both the stopper and trip-lever assemblies, and then scrub them with a brush dipped in white vinegar.

- Grease the moving parts of the assemblies and set them aside.

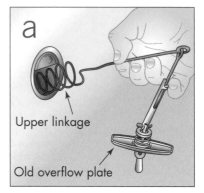

a

Upper linkage

Old overflow plate

THE PROJECT

Warning: Do not use this vinegar-baking soda solution if you've already poured any commercial drain cleaner, bleach, or cleaner down the tub.

1 With the stopper (or strainer) and trip lever removed, pour 1 cup of baking soda down the drain, followed by 1 cup of vinegar. Let this stand for several minutes. It will bubble.

2 Pour a large kettle of boiling water down the drain. Very often, this does the trick. If not, continue with the help of a plunger.

3 Plug the overflow opening (where the trip lever was) with a wet rag.

4 Apply some petroleum jelly to the bottom ring of the plunger.

5 Fill the tub with a few inches of water and start plunging.

6 Once the clog is pushed through, flush the drain with hot water for a few minutes.

7 Reinsert the trip-lever assembly and then the stopper assembly.

8 If the clog is *still* there, see the sidebar "Snake Through Tough Clogs" on page 99.

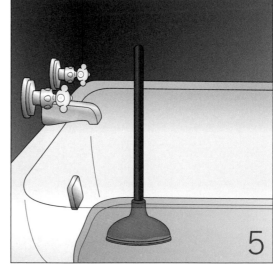

5

Restore Tile and Grout

I like to correct a problem from a least-to most-aggressive approach. Below, I list cleaning mixtures in that order—least aggressive to most aggressive. Examine your tiles and decide which concoction is best for your tile's cleaning needs.

White vinegar, baking soda, salt, commercial tile cleaner, or bleach

Rubber gloves

Safety glasses

Mixing pail and stir stick

Painter's tape

Spray bottle

Small bucket

Nylon scrub brush

Nylon scrubber with handle

Squeegee

Grout sealer

Sponge, rag, or brush

Here's the thing about cleaning tile and grout: The more aggressively you clean them, the less impervious they become (making them more easily stained); hence, the more often they'll need to be cleaned. It's a vicious cycle of tile turmoil. Ugh!

The best medicine for icky tile and grout is prevention. Walls should be sprayed down after each shower with an eco-friendly soap scum/mildew cleaner and preventer like Seventh Generation Shower Cleaner. I also recommend using a squeegee to remove the water because dry walls mean less opportunity for mildew to grow and soap scum to accumulate.

However, if the damage is already done, the following project will blast those tile troublemakers to Timbuktu.

CONSIDER THIS

This project pertains to ceramic and porcelain-glazed tiles. Natural stone tiles require special care because of their porous nature. Use cleaners especially formulated for natural stone, or a solution of water and a few drops of a mild, pH-balanced dishwashing liquid. Also, use a tile-and-grout sealer designed for natural stone.

Some cleaners work best if they're left to sit on the tile surface to saturate the stains. This "sit" time will affect how long it will take to clean and restore tile and grout.

PREP WORK

- Clear away everything from the tub.
- Protect fixture surfaces with painter's tape if recommended by the faucet manufacturer.

- Once you've determined how aggressive you need to get, mix one of the following concoctions:
  - **Vinegar solution.** In a spray bottle, mix one part water with one part vinegar.
  - **Salt/vinegar/baking soda paste.** In a small bucket, mix one part salt, one part baking soda, and one part vinegar.
  - **Bleach paste.** In a pail, mix one part bleach with three parts baking soda.

THE PROJECT

1 Spray or rub your mixture on the entire tile surface. Don't forget to get in all the corners. Allow the product to sit for several minutes. If using the bleach paste, for really tough stains let the product sit for 30 minutes.

2 Scrub the surface with the nylon scrubber.

3 Scrub the grout lines with the nylon brush.

4 Rinse the tiles with fresh water and squeegee them dry.

5 Allow the walls to dry completely, and then apply the grout sealer. Most are painted or rubbed on, but some are sprayed on. Be sure to follow the manufacturer's instructions.

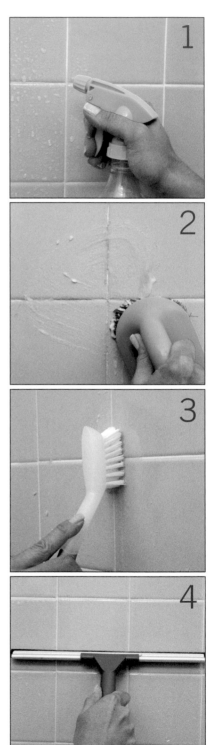

Secure or Replace a Loose or Cracked Soap Dish

If your kids have ever used the soap dish in the tub as a step ladder—*oops!*—they've probably loosened it from the wall. Even dropping one of those industrial drum-size shampoo bottles from a warehouse club could knock loose or even crack a soap dish. Like a loose tile, it's imperative to repair it quickly so that water doesn't get behind it, which would create additional tile damage and cause mold growth.

This project can be applied to various porcelain bath accessories, including towel racks and toothbrush holders.

CONSIDER THIS

The wall behind the tile you're repairing must be dry before you re-glue the soap dish. You can use a hair dryer to speed up the drying time.

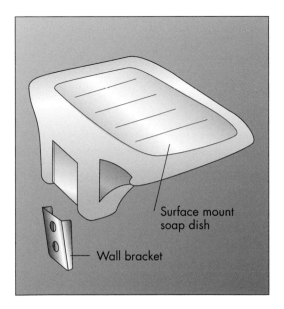

Surface mount soap dish

Wall bracket

You must allow 24 hours of drying time between gluing and grouting/caulking the soap dish before it can get wet or be disturbed. In other words, the tub should be off-limits for 2 days.

You run the risk of breaking surrounding tile when you're prying out the soap dish. Know that you may need to have a replacement tile on hand.

Be careful! Tile shards are very sharp. Where safety gloves and glasses.

Never use a soap dish or towel rack as a grab rail.

PREP WORK

- Plug the drain with a rag and cover basin with a towel or tarp.

- In order to remove the old soap dish, you must first determine how it was mounted. The following two mounting methods are the most common.

  - **Surface Mount:** Accessories that are surface mounted are easily recognized because they sit on the face of the tile, and their placement won't necessarily follow any grout lines. It's mounted to a metal or plastic bracket that is first secured to the wall (see the illustration on the previous page).

    To remove it, break the caulking seal or grout joint with a utility knife (a). Then, with a rubber mallet, gently knock the dish from the bottom up and off of its bracket.

  - **Tile-in:** Typically, this method installs accessories when the walls are being tiled. A tile-in soap dish can be recognized because it's set in place of a tile, so it's not on the tile wall but set "in" it (b).

    To remove a tile-in soap dish, see the project on page 31 in Chapter 2. With a razor scraper, scrape away any silicone or residue on the tile.

THE PROJECT

After you've identified the type of soap dish you have and removed it, here's how to reinstall it. Just be sure that the surface is dry and clean of debris.

SURFACE MOUNT

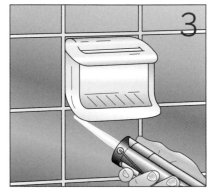

1 With the mounting surface cleared of old adhesive and debris, apply some silicone caulking around the bracket on the wall and then to the back of the dish.

2 Carefully tap the soap dish back on the bracket with a rubber mallet, making sure that it's snug on the bracket. Make sure that it's level. Wait 24 hours before you begin the next step.

3 Caulk or grout around the dish, and wait another 24 hours for the grout or caulk to dry before using the tub.

TILE-IN

1 With the opening clear of debris and any raised bumps of old adhesive, spread a thin coat of tile adhesive on the wall with the short end of a trowel or small putty knife, and then mark grooves in it.

2 On the back of the soap dish, smear a thin layer of adhesive on the grooves.

3 Firmly press the soap dish in place. Wipe away any adhesive that may ooze out of the joints. Make sure that it's level.

4 Place one long strip of masking tape horizontally across the face of the dish, and then two strips vertically over the face of it to secure it to the wall while drying for 24 hours.

5 After drying, remove the tape and grout the joints. Use your finger to smear the grout around the joints. Then wipe away the excess with a damp sponge. Wait another 24 hours for the grout to dry before using the tub.

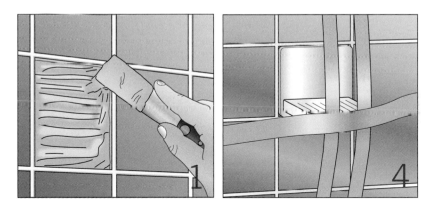

Preventing Bathtub Slips and Falls

Numerous slip-and-fall accidents in showers and tubs occur yearly—often involving trips to the emergency room. These accidents are especially prevalent with seniors and children. I highly recommend using a no-skid product to minimize slipperiness. Though I'm not a big fan of those stick-on decals, some products are very effective and not at all unsightly; NO-Slip Treatment is one of them. It increases grip by bonding microscopic particles to a surface, but it will not visibly change the color or texture. A no-skid product can be applied to many floors as well and is a total do-it-yourself project.

Toilets

A toilet that's clogged or won't flush can send an entire household into a panic. Usually the fix is as simple as a push of a plunger or the twist of a pair of pliers. Find these and other simple toilet fixes in this chapter.

Replace a Toilet Seat

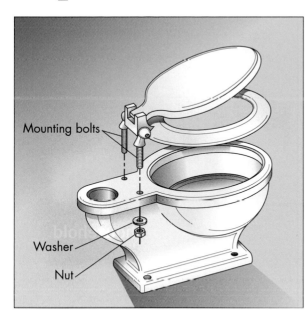

Mounting bolts

Washer

Nut

Nothing screams "disgusting" more than a cruddy old toilet seat. I remember once sitting on one that scarred me, literally. Although it wasn't dirty, it did have a hairline crack in it. The crack slit open as I sat down, and then pinched closed right on my butt cheek. *Ouch!*

Promise me you won't subject anyone to disgust or pain when they use your toilet. This project is very basic, so if your toilet seat is less than perfect, change it!

WHAT YOU'LL NEED

Replacement toilet seat
Flathead screwdriver
Adjustable wrench*
Mini hacksaw*
Disinfectant cleaner
Rag
Lubricating spray*
Duct tape*
* If applicable

a

CONSIDER THIS

When choosing a new seat, the only thing you need to know in advance is whether your toilet is round or elongated. You can purchase a custom fit and color seat from your toilet's manufacturer, but they typically cost more.

PREP WORK

- Remove the old seat by unscrewing the mounting bolts (a). They're sometimes hidden behind plastic caps. If applicable, pry up the caps with a flathead screwdriver and unscrew the bolts. Depending on your seat type, you remove the bolt by unscrewing the nuts from underneath.

- Unscrew the bolts completely, remove the old washers and nuts, and lift out the seat.

- If the bolts are just spinning but not unscrewing, you'll need to hold back the nut from underneath with an adjustable wrench.

- If the bolts are rusty and stubborn, spray them with lubricating spray and let them soak for several minutes. Then go back and give it a whirl.

• If the bolts are truly stuck, they may need to be cut off with a mini hacksaw. Use duct tape to protect areas that may be hit with the saw as you're sawing off the old bolts.

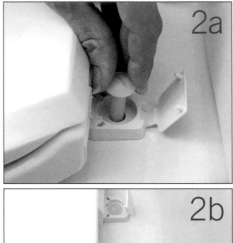

2a

THE PROJECT

1 Clean up around the bolt holes with disinfectant cleaner. Lubricating spray does well here to remove rusty crud.

2 With the seat closed, lift up the caps (if applicable), line up the bolts (a), and slip them through the holes (b). Some seats provide small foam pads to prevent seat wiggling. If so, stack them around the bolt holes.

3 Slip the washer and nut onto the bolt and hand-screw them snug. Be careful not to over-tighten—doing so can crack the porcelain.

4 If the bolt is slotted, hold back the nut with the wrench and tighten the bolt with a screwdriver. Do not over-tighten.

5 If applicable, snap the caps closed.

6 Open and close the cover. It should move freely, but not wiggle. Adjust if necessary.

2b

3

Mini Hacksaw Heaven

I love this tool! A close quarter hacksaw like the one shown here has been a lifesaver for me. I was once replacing old faucets in my mom's house in Vegas. The water there is so bad; it corroded the fittings to the point that practically every faucet had to be cut out. I couldn't have done the job without that mini hacksaw getting into all the hard-to-reach spots. And it surprisingly cuts through metal like *buttah!*

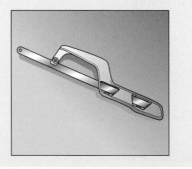

(DVD) Replace a Flush Handle

WHAT YOU'LL NEED

Replacement handle

Adjustable wrench or tongue-and-groove pliers

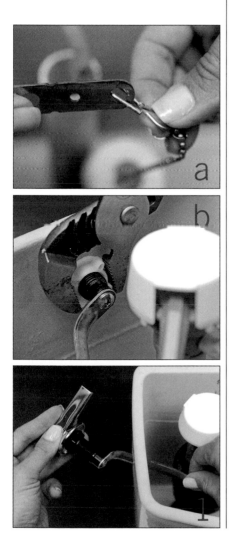

I'm no superman, but I've managed to crack a plastic flush handle right off the toilet. (It happened to be on the first visit to my boyfriend's house—wasn't I embarrassed.) Whether it's broken or you just want it to match your new oil-bronzed faucet and towel rack, replacing a flush handle is as simple as it gets.

CONSIDER THIS

Be sure to bring the old flush handle with you to the plumbing supply store for a proper replacement. The length of the trip arm and size and shape of the handle (that fits in the toilet cutout) must match perfectly in order for the handle to work properly. Why mess with trying to alter the cutout or length of the arm when you can just buy the right one from the start?

PREP WORK

- To remove the old handle, you need to know this tidbit—the fitting on a flush handle has *reverse threads*. This means that in order to unscrew it, you need to turn the fitting clockwise, not counterclockwise. (So the *lefty loosey, righty tighty* rule goes out the window!)
- First, lift the chain or disconnect the wire off of the lift arm (**a**).
- Unscrew the handle nut, *clockwise,* with your wrench or pliers (b).
- Pull out the handle and lift arm and take the entire assembly to the plumbing store to buy a replacement.

THE PROJECT

1 Insert the new lift arm through the hole.

2 Screw the nut, counterclockwise, onto the handle.

3 Reattach the chain or wire to the lift arm.

4 Flush and adjust the wire or chain if necessary.

Toilet Maintenance

WHAT YOU'LL NEED

Steel wool

All materials necessary to empty the tank
(see the Prep Work section on page 100)

There are several little maintenance tips you should know about to keep your toilet fresh and up and running—or should I say *not* running, as in the annoying jiggle-the-handle kind.

THE PROJECT: Cleaning the valve seat

Sometimes all that's causing the toilet to run is a faulty seal around the valve seat. Over time, gunk will form around the valve seat and flapper. This will not allow the flapper to seal properly, which will cause the water to run out of the tank into the bowl when it's not supposed to.

PREP WORK

In order to do this project, you need to work with an empty tank. Follow the steps in the Prep Work section on page 100.

1 With the tank empty, lift the flapper to review the valve seat. Pull off the flapper from the overflow tube; it may be hooked in place with "wings" on either side of it or have a large thick ring that will be pulled up and over the tube.

2 Scrub the entire lip of the valve seat with steel wool.

3 Scrub the underside of the flapper.

4 Reattach the flapper to the overflow tube.

5 Turn the water back on and give it a flush.

THE PROJECT: Cleaning the flush holes

Is your flush sluggish? It could be because not enough water is flushing through the bowl in one shot, which is necessary for a good, strong flush. Especially in areas with hard water, mineral deposits will clog the flush holes, making for a wimpy flush.

WHAT YOU'LL NEED

Rubber gloves**

Safety glasses

White vinegar in a spray bottle

Nylon scrub brush

Handheld mirror

Wire hanger

**Optional

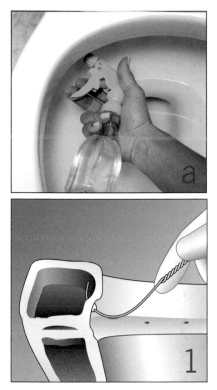

PREP WORK

- Shut off the water to the tank from the shut-off valve and flush the toilet; you don't want water to dilute the vinegar.

- Spray the entire underside of the bowl rim (where the flush rings are) with vinegar. With the sprayer in the "stream" position, spray the vinegar into the holes (a).

- Let the vinegar soak for an hour.

1 Fish the hook of the wire hanger in and out of each hole to unclog the debris. Use the mirror if you're having difficulty seeing them.

2 Scrub the entire underside of the bowl rim with the brush, dipping it in vinegar as you work.

3 Turn the water back on and flush.

4 Repeat from Step 1 if more unclogging is needed.

WHAT YOU'LL NEED

Borax
Lemon juice
Small bucket
Scouring pad
Toilet pumice stone
Rubber gloves*
**Optional

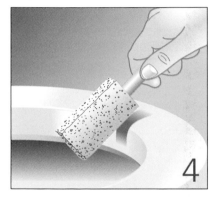

THE PROJECT: Eliminating stains and water rings

Here's an all-purpose cleaner that eliminates tons of toilet tarnishes—from rust to lime scale.

PREP WORK

- Shut off the water to the tank from the shut-off valve and flush the toilet; you don't want water to dilute the cleaning solution.

- Mix equal parts borax and lemon juice to make a paste.

1 With a scouring pad, rub the borax/lemon-juice paste all around the bowl.

2 Let it soak for an hour.

3 Flush the bowl and see if all the stains are gone.

4 If stains remain, use a toilet pumice stone with some more paste to scrub those stubborn stains away.

Plunge a Toilet

WHAT YOU'LL NEED

Toilet plunger (also known as a flange or ball plunger)

Rubber gloves

Bucket*

* If applicable

It's a nasty job, but somebody's got to do it.

CONSIDER THIS

Do not try to plunge a bowl that is almost full. Wait for the water to drain down before starting to plunge.

PREP WORK

The rubber of the plunger should be covered with water to work best. Add water to the bowl if necessary.

THE PROJECT

1 Lift the toilet seat and insert the funnel of the plunger deep into the drain outlet so that it creates a seal.

2 Thrust the plunger up and down rapidly, being sure to create strong suction and pressure. After doing this several times, swiftly pull the plunger up and out of the water.

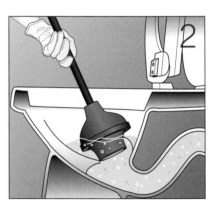

3 Continue doing this until the clog breaks and the water begins to go down.

4 Test to see if the clog is cleared by pouring a bucket of water down the bowl. I like a bucket better than flushing because if you try to flush at this point and it's not really unclogged yet, you run the risk of the bowl overflowing (unless you quickly shut off the water from the valve).

5 Continue plunging if it's still not cleared.

6 If the clog is persistent, see the sidebar, "Snake Through Tough Clogs" on page 99.

Walls and Floors

Small fixes like patched drywall holes and newly stained floor grout are not much of an investment, but wow, what a difference. Check out how projects like these can refresh the look and function of your bathroom.

Patch Holes in Drywall

WHAT YOU'LL NEED

Newspaper or old towel
Utility knife
4-inch putty knife
Nylon mesh tape
Spackle
Fine sandpaper

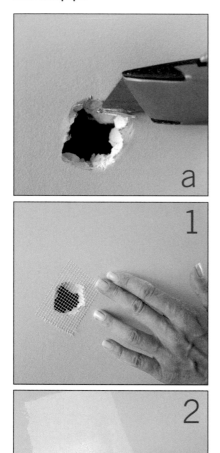

I find that holes in bathroom walls are prevalent. Towel bars loosen and pull out. So do toilet-paper holders, shower rods, decorative objects, shelf placements—there are lots of opportunities for holes to pop up all around the bathroom. I recently patched a hole in my master bath when I changed the position of the light fixture over my vanity (see the "Matching Wall Texture" sidebar on the next page).

THE PROJECT: Patching small holes (1–3 inches)

PREP WORK

- Put down newspaper or an old towel to protect the floor beneath the hole.
- With the utility knife, cut out any bits of drywall that are protruding out of the hole (a).
- Lightly scuff up the painted area around the hole with the sandpaper (about an inch around).

1 Place a piece of nylon mesh tape over the hole. For very small holes (like from a screw and plastic anchor), this step is not necessary.

2 With a dab of spackle on your putty knife, smear the spackle over the hole and tape.

3 Smooth out the spackle and let it dry. If, when it's dry, you see that another coat is needed, sand lightly and pass another coat.

4 When it's completely dry, sand any raised edges, prime, and paint.

WHAT YOU'LL NEED

4-inch putty knife and plaster trowel
Speed Square
Utility knife
Drywall saw
Newspaper or old towel
Level and pencil
Tape measure
Scrap square of drywall
Joint compound
Fine sandpaper

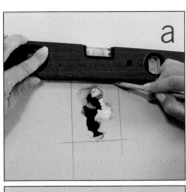

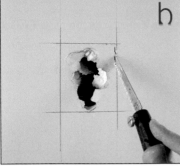

THE PROJECT: Patching medium holes (4–6 inches)

This patch has many names—hot patch, hat patch, and blow patch are some of them.

PREP WORK

- Put down newspaper or an old towel to protect the floor beneath the hole.

- With a level to mark straight lines (a), cut out a clean square around the hole with a drywall saw (b). Lightly scuff up the painted area around the square with the sandpaper (about an inch around).

- Take the measurements of the square opening, add 1½ inches to each side, and then trace and cut a scrap piece of drywall to those dimensions.

1 Place your square drywall patch face down and, with a T-square, trace out the dimension of the square hole.

2 Score the lines with a utility knife, and then bend and crack the drywall rock. Now peel the rock off the paper. Do this to each side. You'll be left with what looks like a square hat that has a 1½-inch brim.

Matching Wall Texture

Okay, so you made a wall patch—excellent. But what do you do if the wall is textured? How do you reestablish that finish? Many walls have an orange-peel texture that may seem impossible to re-create. The good news is that two products on the market are available for this very purpose.

Spray texture. This product comes in a spray can with different-size nozzles to establish medium to heavy textures. Basically, you spray it over the patch, let it set up, and then knock it down with a putty knife. Follow the manufacturer's instructions.

Adhesive texture patch. This product is perfect for small patches under 3 inches. I especially like this method for areas that aren't in a "bump" zone. The product claims that you don't even need to spackle the hole. You just choose from one of the light- to heavy-textured patches and stick it over the hole—done. Personally, I'm more comfortable giving the hole a smear of spackle first. I recently used this patch over a drywall repair to conceal a hole from a switched-out light fixture over my vanity—it's next to impossible to find the patch.

3 Test to see that the patch fits snugly in the hole—adjust if necessary.

4 With a putty knife, smear a generous layer of joint compound all around each side of the hole.

5 Press the patch into the hole and smooth the "brim" down with the putty knife.

6 As the mud squeezes out from behind the brim, spread it over the entire surface of the patch.

7 With the trowel, pass more mud over the entire surface of the patch. Let it dry.

8 Sand any raised edges and pass another coat, being sure to feather out the edges. This step may need to be repeated.

9 When it's completely dry, sand smooth, prime, and paint.

WHAT YOU'LL NEED

Drill/driver

Speed Square

Utility knife

Drywall saw

4-inch putty knife and plaster trowel

Newspaper or old towel

Level and pencil

Tape measure

Scrap square of drywall (match the thickness of your wall—usually ½ inch)

2, two-by-four lengths of wood

1⅝-inch drywall screws

Joint compound

Fine sandpaper

THE PROJECT: Patching large holes (smaller than 8 inches)

PREP WORK

- Put down newspaper or an old towel to protect the floor beneath the hole.

- With a level to mark straight lines, cut out a clean square around the hole. Lightly scuff up the painted area around the square with the sandpaper (about an inch around).

- Take the measurements of the square opening, and then trace and cut a scrap piece of drywall to those dimensions (cut on the inside of the pencil line so the square is slightly smaller than the hole). Now you have your patch square.

- Cut a length of two-by-four, 4 inches longer than the hole.

1 Insert the first two-by-four into the hole. Line up the flat side of the two-by-four on one side of the opening.

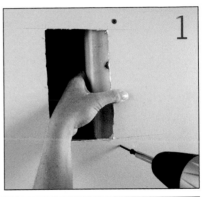

2 Secure the two-by-four to the wall by driving a screw into the two-by-four above and below the hole. **Note:** For a smaller hole (6–8 inches), one two-by-four centered in the opening will suffice. Drive a screw halfway in the middle of the two-by-four to use as a handle so that it doesn't drop behind the drywall as you're screwing it in place.

3 Secure the second two-by-four to the other side of the opening in the same manner.

4 Insert the patch square into the hole and screw it to the two-by-fours with a couple of screws on each side.

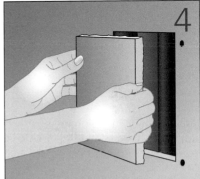

5 Put nylon mesh tape over each joint (a) and, with a putty knife, smear joint compound over each seam (b). Let it dry.

6 Sand any raised edges and pass another coat of joint compound over the entire patch, being sure to feather out the edges. Once dry, repeat this step for your final coat.

7 When it's completely dry, sand smooth, prime, and paint.

Tighten a Loose Towel Bar or Toilet-Paper Holder

WHAT YOU'LL NEED

Set of Allen wrench (hex keys) **or jeweler's screwdriver depending on your type of set-screw**

Handheld mirror

All too often, bars and holders in the bathroom start to jiggle over time, especially in a bathroom that gets a lot of action.

CONSIDER THIS

There are several ways to install towel bars and toilet-paper holders. Today, most have mounting brackets that the unit is fastened to; this project addresses this type of bar and holder.

If your bar or holder has loosened because the mounting bracket has pulled out from the wall, the project gets a bit more complicated. The brackets will need to be remounted in fresh holes (see "Install Grab Bars or Hand Grips" on page 111.

THE PROJECT

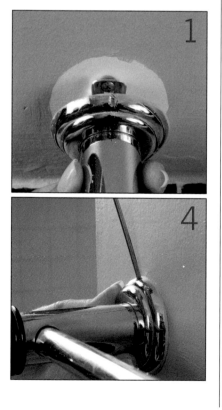

1. Locate the set-screw, which is usually hidden at the bottom of the decorative cover. The photo shows the top of the cover.

2. Peek under and see if it's a hex-type or flathead-type set screw—the mirror can help here.

3. If it's a hex type, fit test various hex keys to see which one is the right size.

4. Turn the set-screw counterclockwise (from an underneath orientation) and tighten it back onto the mounting bracket. This may take loosening the screw first, adjusting the cover so that it sits properly on the bracket, and then retightening the set-screw.

Secure a Loose or Hollow Floor Tile

WHAT YOU'LL NEED

Drill/driver

⅛-inch masonry bit

Rubber mallet

Vacuum

Tile-repair adhesive (elastomer type)

Caulking gun

Rag

Heavy object (like a toolbox or bucket filled with water)

Matching grout and grouting materials (see the "What You'll Need" list on page 31)

Sometimes a floor tile will loosen or sound hollow simply because the adhesive failed. Here's a quick fix for the innocent kind of loose.

CONSIDER THIS

This repair will take at least 48 hours before the tile can be walked on. Read the manufacturer's instructions for product drying times.

The adhesive used in this project is not for use in wet areas like showers or pools.

Playing the Grout Color-Match Game

When doing a spot repair on tile, matching grout color is daunting. Even with the same brand and color, old and new grout just won't match. Grout darkens over time due to wear and reactions with cleaning products. So the very same color will be lighter than what is already on your floor. In this case, why not just start with a darker-patch color? Well, yes, that will match . . . at first. But remember that, over time, that will darken too, becoming darker than the existing grout. Ugh! Of course, degrees of this darkening will vary. Bottom line is, matching grout is just not a perfect science. With that in mind, here are some tips on how to be a successful grout matchmaker:

- Scrub your existing tiles to brighten the grout and get its truest color (see "Restore Tile and Grout" on page 39).
- Bring home a grout color chart and find the closest match.
- You may need to mix two colors to get the right match.
- If you know that your existing grout has darkened a lot since its installation, choose a color that is slightly lighter than what's there (knowing that it will darken with time—catching up to the color of the existing grout). Don't go so light that the contrast is an eyesore.
- Know that dry grout, like paint, is the best representation of the color.
- You can use a grout stain and alter the grout color of the entire floor to ensure best uniformity (see "Stain and Seal Floor Grout" on page 61).

PREP WORK

Tap around the tile with the mallet and identify what part of the tile is loose or hollow (a).

THE PROJECT

1 Drill holes in the grout joints around the tile, concentrating around the area that is failing. Be careful not to drill the tile itself. Drill slightly past the tile depth—you'll probably feel once you've gone through the grout. Four to eight holes will suffice.

2 Vacuum out all loose debris—actually put the vacuum nozzle over each hole.

3 Inject the repair adhesive directly into each hole by putting the tip right down into the drilled hole. Tap the tile with the mallet to ensure the product is settling deep in there.

4 Wipe away any excess with a wet rag.

5 Place a heavy object over the tile and follow the recommended drying time. Be sure to follow all manufacturer's instructions.

6 When completely dry, grout with matching grout color (see the sidebar on the previous page).

Replace a Broken Floor Tile

WHAT YOU'LL NEED

Floor tile

Masonry chisel and hammer

Rubber mallet

Notched trowel

Grout saw

Scraper

Newspaper

Masking tape

Small old towel

Safety glasses and gloves

Vacuum

Thin-set mortar

Mixing pail and stir stick

Rag

Matching grout and grouting materials
(see the "What You'll Need" list on page 31)

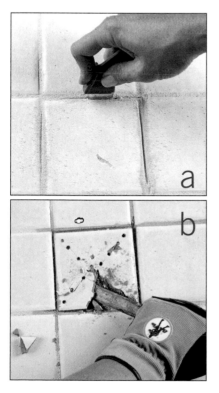

For me, it was a solid brass antique gaslight valve my cousin Sal gave me—he knows I go crazy over stuff like that. When he found it in rubble on a remodeling job, he knew I'd love it. Boy, did I! It went right on a shelf in my bathroom where I proudly display my other antique hardware pieces. Wouldn't you know it? While dusting, I knocked the gaslight right off the shelf onto the tile floor. Happily, my antique valve was without a scratch. My floor tile, on the other hand . . . well, that was a different story. Here's the fix.

CONSIDER THIS

This repair will take at least 48 hours before anyone can walk on the tile. Read the manufacturer's instructions for product drying times.

PREP WORK

- You can protect the surrounding tiles by masking them off with newspaper.

- Saw out the grout around the broken tile with the grout saw (a).

- Drill several holes in the tile in an X shape and chisel out pieces of the tile (b). Use the hammer and chisel to break out the tile. Start where the broken section is and work out from there. Be sure to wear safety glasses and gloves, and use solid blows.

- Clear out any remaining bits of mortar with a scraper. Be careful not to damage the substrate (the base that the tile is adhered to).

- Vacuum out any debris.

THE PROJECT

1 In a pail, mix the thin-set according to the manufacturer's instructions.

2 With the short end of the notched trowel, spread the mortar along the back of the replacement tile. Don't go all the way to the edges. Spread the mortar on the floor as well.

3 Place *buttered tile* (a tile with thin-set mortar on the back side) into the space, being sure to leave equal spacing all around it.

4 Tap the tile gently with a rubber mallet so that the tile is level and flush with the surrounding tiles.

5 Wipe away any mortar that may have oozed out with a wet rag.

6 Let it dry for 24 hours.

7 When it's completely dry, grout it with matching grout color (see the sidebar "Playing the Grout Color-Match Game" on page 57).

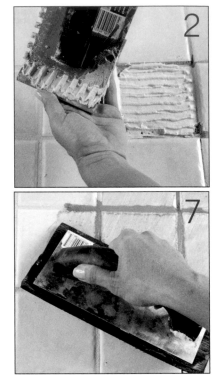

Stain and Seal Floor Grout

WHAT YOU'LL NEED

Grout stain and sealant product
Toothbrush
Shallow container
Clean rag

Okay, so you've tried my scrubbing tips on the floor (see page 40), but the grout is still less than lovely. Don't give up yet! Using a grout stain and seal (both products in one), give the grout a uniform fresh color that will rejuvenate your floor.

CONSIDER THIS

If you have recently done a tile patch, you must wait the total cure time—usually at least 7 days—before attempting to stain the grout. Follow the grout manufacturer's instructions for cure time.

Grout stain usually dries within hours, and normal traffic is permitted within the day. However, total cure time maybe over 7 days.

Unless otherwise indicated, these stains are *not* for use on natural stone or porous tiles.

You must follow the grout stain manufacturer's instructions for full knowledge of use and safety precautions for the product.

PREP WORK

- Grout must be completely clean and dry. It must also be free of pre-applied coatings of wax or sealant.

- To ensure color choice, do a patch test on a hidden section of tile.

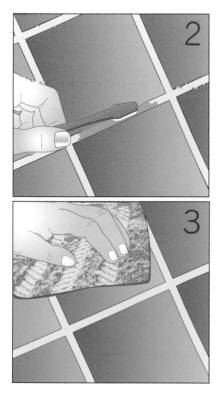

THE PROJECT

1 Shake the closed bottle of stain, and then pour some in a shallow container.

2 Dip the toothbrush in the stain and brush it into the grout joints. Work in small sections.

3 When the product is "set up" in the joints, but still wet on the tile, wipe away any excess stain from the tile with a dry rag.

4 It usually takes a week for the product to cure. Normal traffic is permitted during this time, but do not clean or wet it.

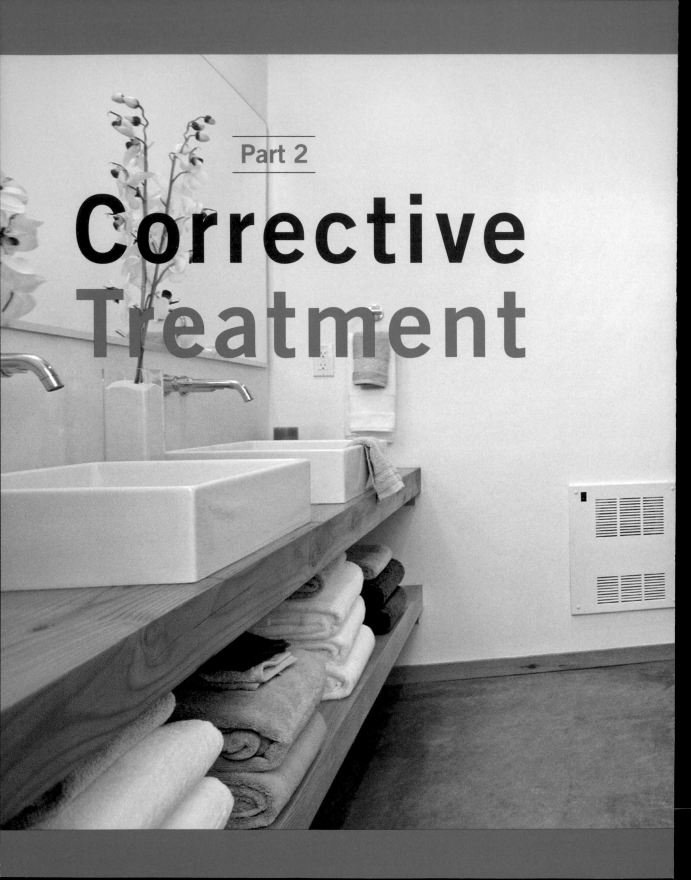

Part 2

Corrective Treatment

Sinks

An adjustable tilt mirror and a new vanity light above the sink may be just the right changes to give your bathroom a new look. Stopping that annoying faucet drip may be just the right fix to give you a little peace and quiet.

Repair a Leaky Faucet

WHAT YOU'LL NEED

The following tools should be on hand for any of the faucet-type fixes in this section.

Flathead and Phillips screwdrivers

Adjustable wrench

Tongue-and-groove pliers

Needle-nose pliers

Allen wrenches (hex keys)

Cartridge puller (for cartridge type only)*

Clean rag

Metal nail file*

Masking tape

Penetrating oil

Heat-resistant plumber's grease

Steel wool or scouring sponge

Flashlight

Faucet repair kit, washers, O-rings, cartridges, discs, and so on (depending on your type of faucet)

Valve seat wrench or seat dresser (for compression type only)

Plastic bag

* If applicable

When looking to fix that irritating and wasteful *plip-plip* from the bathroom faucet, the first thing you must do is identify which type of faucet it is from an internal standpoint. In general, there are four faucet types: *compression, ball, cartridge,* and *disk.* These names actually depict the part that controls the water flow.

You can make an educated guess as to which type of faucet you'll need based on characteristics mentioned in this section. An easy way to identify which type you have is to contact the manufacturer. Being the adventurous type, I like to just open up the faucet (which you'd have to do anyway) and take a look around. It makes me feel like a doctor doing exploratory surgery.

CONSIDER THIS

You must locate and check that your faucet shut-off valves are working properly before starting this project. These faucet repairs require that you shut the water off from the water supply shut-off valve. These shut-offs are usually located under the sink—one for the hot and one for the cold. If you ever want to experience firsthand an *I Love Lucy* calamity, unscrew the faucet handle and start to dismantle the parts without shutting the water off from the valves. Water will start shooting out and into your face like a geyser.

Once the water is off at the shut-off valves, slightly turn on the faucet to verify that it's completely off and to release the pressure.

Note that your faucet may vary slightly from what is described and illustrated.

Remember to keep track of the order in which parts are disassembled to help you when you're putting them back together.

PREP WORK

These steps apply to all of the following faucet-type fixes:

- Shut off the water to the faucet from the shut-off valves. This step is imperative to avoid a flood.

- Close the stopper and place a rag in the sink so that nothing falls down the drain and it's protected.

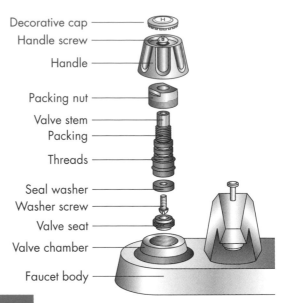

Decorative cap
Handle screw
Handle
Packing nut
Valve stem
Packing
Threads
Seal washer
Washer screw
Valve seat
Valve chamber
Faucet body

THE PROJECT: Compression-type faucet

The compression-type faucet is the oldest, most common, and least expensive of the four. It has two control handles. A stem with an affixed washer raises and lowers to open and close the water valve as you turn each handle. What usually needs repair on this type of faucet is the washer and/or *valve seat,* which gets worn out from the compression and grinding.

Know that you may have a choice on how to proceed with this fix. You can either repair the old valve assembly or replace it with a new replacement cartridge—some manufacturers are now offering this as an option. Check online or with your plumbing supply store about a replacement cartridge for your compression-type faucet. If the cartridge is available, go with it! Though it will be more expensive initially, cartridges last much longer than seats and washers. Just follow Steps 1, 2, 3, and 5, and then insert the cartridge.

1 With the water shut off from the shut-off valves, remove the handles. To do this you must locate a screw that is usually hidden beneath a decorative cap. Gently pry the cap off with a metal nail file or flathead screwdriver. With the screw exposed, unscrew it and lift off the handle.

2 Locate the packing or retaining nut. With tongue-and-groove pliers or an adjustable wrench, turning counterclockwise, unscrew the packing nut and put it to the side.

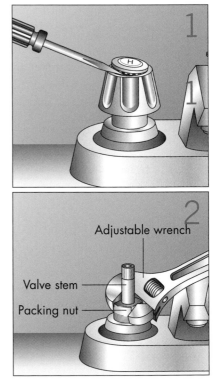

Adjustable wrench
Valve stem
Packing nut

3 With the valve stem now exposed, pop the handle back on the stem, and use it to easily unscrew the valve assembly up and out of the valve chamber.

4 On the bottom of the valve stem, you'll see that the washer is screwed in place by a single brass screw. It will likely be split and corroded. It may have even broken off and is sitting in the valve chamber. It's best to take the entire assembly to the plumbing store for the correct washer replacement.

5 In addition to new washers, you should examine the valve seat. Run your finger along it to see if there are bumps that would prevent a tight seal (a). If there are imperfections it must be corrected by either replacing or redressing the valve seat, which will depend on the type of seat you have.

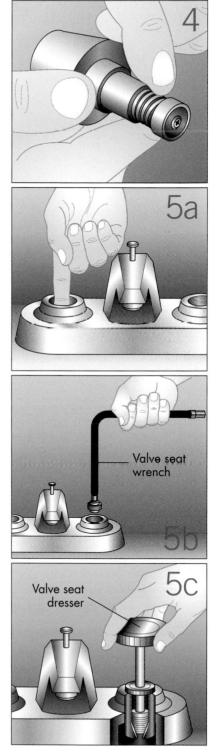

- The replaceable valve seat will have a hex or slotted shape in its center. You'll need a *valve-seat wrench* to unscrew it. Insert the wrench and unscrew the valve seat (b). Bring it to the store for replacement.

- The fixed-type valve seat will have a simple round hole in it. You'll need a *valve seat dresser* to resurface the seat. Insert the seat dresser into the chamber and give it a few spins to "dress" the seat (c). Do so until the seat looks shiny. Be sure to wipe away the metal shavings with a rag once it's dressed.

6 With steel wool or a scrubber, clean the valve stem.

7 Screw on the new washer, being sure that it's snug, but not deformed.

8 Hand-screw the valve stem back into the chamber and then reinstall the retaining nut with pliers or a wrench.

9 Pop the handles back on, but don't screw them on yet. Turn the water back on and make sure the handles and faucet are not leaking. Screw on the handles, snap on the caps, and you're done!

THE PROJECT: Ball-type faucet

A ball-type faucet always has a single control handle. A hollow metal or plastic ball rotates as you turn the handle that controls the mixture and volume of the hot and cold water. It has many little parts and for this reason more opportunities for leaks.

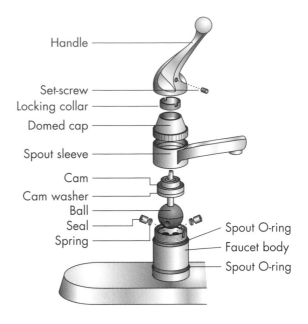

Handle
Set-screw
Locking collar
Domed cap
Spout sleeve
Cam
Cam washer
Ball
Seal
Spring
Spout O-ring
Faucet body
Spout O-ring

1 With the water shut off from the shut-off valves, remove the handle. Locate the set-screw in the handle housing. It's sometimes hidden behind a small decorative cover. Pry off the cover with a flathead screwdriver or metal nail file, loosen the set-screw with an Allen wrench, and lift off the handle.

2 If the leak is coming from the bottom of the handle, you may just need to tighten the locking collar (adjusting collar). Use the wrench that is included in the ball-type repair kit (it's a *spanner wrench*) to tighten the collar by turning it clockwise. To test if this has done the trick, turn on the water from the shut-off valve and see if this has corrected the leak. If it has, you're done. Just screw the handle back on. If not, you'll need to disassemble the rest of the faucet.

3 Make sure to shut the water back off at the shut-off valve to continue. Loosen the collar with the spanner wrench. Now remove the domed cap. First wrap the jaws of the pliers with masking tape to protect the finish on the cap, and then twist and pull off the domed cap.

4 Lift out the cam and the cam washer, and then the ball by its stem.

5 Your best bet is to replace all of these parts because you have the faucet apart anyway—the kit should have everything you need. Use penetrating oil around all the threads and parts to clean them off before replacing and reassembling the parts.

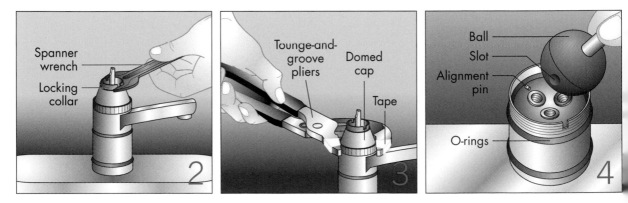

Spanner wrench
Locking collar
2

Tounge-and-groove pliers
Domed cap
Tape
3

Ball
Slot
Alignment pin
O-rings
4

6 With needle-nose pliers or a flathead screwdriver, pull out the valve seats and springs from inside the faucet. Be aware that these little parts will try to roll away from you.

7 Slip the new seats and springs onto the tip of a screwdriver and drop them down into position—tap them in place with your finger. Note that the springs go in first, and then the cupped side of the seats fit over the springs.

8 If the faucet is leaking at the base, it's probably the O-rings that need replacing. Pull off the spout with your masking-taped pliers and examine the O-rings. Pry them off with the hooked end of the spanner wrench or screwdriver. Put plumber's grease around the new O-rings and roll them back in place.

9 Reassemble all the parts. Insert the new ball, cam washer, and cam—make sure that any tabs and notches line up with one another.

10 Slip on the domed cap, tighten the collar with the spanner wrench. Screw on the handle and pop in the decorative cover.

11 Turn on the water from the shut-off valve and check for leaks. Nice job!

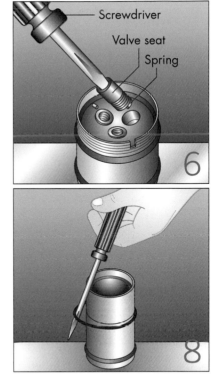

THE PROJECT: Cartridge-type faucet

A cartridge-type faucet (my favorite) uses a plastic or brass cartridge that houses a stem that slides up and down in the handle to control the water flow. They're used in single- or double-handled faucets. It's the simplest of all types to work on because the entire cartridge slips in and out for easy repair or replacement.

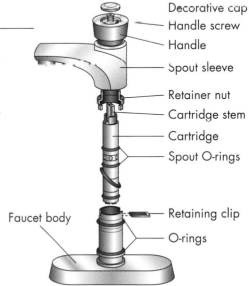

1 With the water shut off from the shut-off valves, remove the handle(s). To do this you must locate a screw that is usually hidden beneath a decorative cap. Gently pry the cap off with a metal nail file or flathead screwdriver (a). With the screw exposed, unscrew it and lift off the handle (b).

2 With the handle off, there may be a sleeve, locking nut, and/or retaining clip(s) that need to be removed. Use a wrench or needle-nose pliers to remove the sleeve or nut. Use a flathead screwdriver or pliers to remove the clip. (Faucets vary, so you may need to work through a bit of a puzzle to remove the cap, handle, nut, clip(s), and so on—be patient!)

3 Pull out the cartridge using pliers, but first look to see if there's a mark, flat side, or notch and mentally note its orientation. Pulling out the cartridge may take some patience—wiggle it out little by little. If the cartridge puller won't budge, see the sidebar "Using a Cartridge Puller" on page 86.

4 Examine the O-rings. If the cartridge doesn't show corrosion, but the O-rings look worn, simply replace the O-rings. Use a flathead screwdriver to pry them off. Put plumber's grease around the new O-rings and roll them back in place.

5 To replace the cartridge, bring the old one to the store with you for the proper replacement part. Remember to note the brand of faucet. If you have a choice of brass or plastic, opt for brass—although more expensive, it lasts much longer.

6 To insert the new cartridge first recall a mark, flat side, or notch to indicate orientation. Push the new cartridge in place with your finger. The manufacturer may recommend plumber's grease.

7 Reassemble the unit—insert the retaining clip(s), locking nut, and so on (if applicable), and then reattach the handle.

8 Turn on the water from the shut-off valve and test the faucet for leaks. If it's a single-handle control, check to see that hot and cold water work in the proper handle position. If they're crossed (hot comes out of cold and vice versa), rotate the cartridge 180 degrees.

9 Replace the decorative cap. Finished!

THE PROJECT: Disc-type faucet

A disc-type faucet is usually a single-handled control as illustrated in this project. They work like this— in a cylinder, two disks, either plastic or ceramic, glide over one another as you spin the handle. Each disk has corresponding holes that open and close as they rotate to control the flow of hot and cold water. They're practically maintenance free. But, if you have hard water, seals may corrode or a disk may crack.

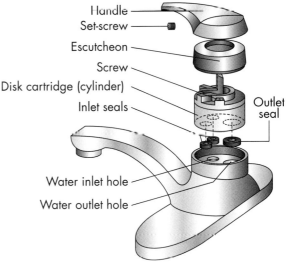

Handle —
Set-screw —
Escutcheon —
Screw —
Disk cartridge (cylinder) —
Inlet seals —
Outlet seal
Water inlet hole —
Water outlet hole —

1 With the water shut off from the shut-off valves, remove the handle. Locate the set-screw in the handle housing. It's sometimes hidden behind a small decorative cover. Pry off the cover with a flathead screwdriver or metal nail file, loosen the set-screw with an Allen wrench, and lift off the handle.

2 Lift off the escutcheon, which should expose the disk assembly (also referred to as the disk cartridge or cylinder).

3 You'll probably see mounting screws.Unscrew them and lift out the cylinder—use pliers if it's stubborn.

4 With the disk assembly out, you'll see three neoprene seals. Remove them and clean off any debris in the recesses or on the lower disk with a plastic scour pad.

5 Insert the new seals. A cleaned disk, inlets, and new seals may be all you need to stop the leak. To check if this has done the trick, reassemble the faucet, and put the handle in the on position. Then slowly turn on the water from the shut-off—a sudden surge of water could crack a disk.

6 If there's still a leak, shut off the water from the shut-off valve and disassemble the faucet as described in Steps 1–4.

7 With the entire disk assembly removed, drop in the new replacement cartridge and reassemble the faucet and screw on the handle.

8 Put the handle in the on position, and then slowly turn on the water from the shut-off valve. Give the faucet a spin, check for leaks . . . *tah-dah!*

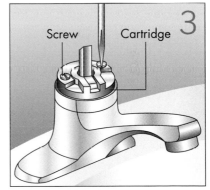

Screw   Cartridge   3

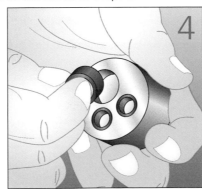

4

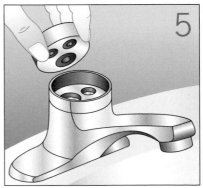

5

Renew a Cultured Marble Vanity Countertop

WHAT YOU'LL NEED

This process is also used on cars and boats. You can readily find these materials in an auto parts or marine store.

Electric drill or buffer/polisher

Masking tape

Newspaper

Dust mask

Safety glasses

1200-grit wet/dry sandpaper

Sponge

Bucket of water

Clean rags

Buffing pads that fit an electric drill or electric buffer/polisher

Rubbing compound for fiberglass (medium cutting)

Microfiber towel

Paste wax or polish for fiberglass

Sponge or foam pad for paste or polish

Many vanity countertops are made of cultured marble (also known as engineered marble). Cultured marble is actually a composite of marble dust or crushed limestone and polyester resins. It requires less care than a tile or natural stone countertop. However, over time, it can lose its shine and start to look dull and shabby.

Renewing cultured marble is a matter of restoring the *gelcoat finish.* This top coat is applied during the manufacturing process in order to create a shiny, waterproof surface. When this gelcoat gets scratched or discolored, it can be sanded, rubbed, and then buffed to look like new.

CONSIDER THIS

- I recommend removing the faucet so it's out of your way. (See "Installing a New Faucet and Pop-up" on page 125.)
- Deep scratches and stains that have gone through the gelcoat are impossible to remove. Do not sand past the gelcoat! Doing so will leave a permanent dull spot.
- All the steps can be done by hand. However, a buffer/polisher is optimal because it rotates evenly and at a low speed (unlike a drill).
- If you use a drill/driver with a buffing pad, be careful not to overdo it—controlling the speed is the key.
- To maintain your cultured countertop, regularly use a product like Gel-Gloss to keep a waterproof and shiny surface.

PREP WORK

- Remove the faucet (see the Prep Work section on page 126).
- Protect the surrounding area by taping it off with newspaper.

THE PROJECT

1 Wrap the sandpaper around the sponge and dip it in water.

2 Begin sanding the surface using a swirling motion. Concentrate on deep scratches and stains, but do not over-sand. Continue dipping in water and sanding the entire countertop.

3 Rinse the entire surface with water, being sure to remove any sanding debris.

4 Use the drill with a buffing pad or buffer/polisher to apply the rubbing compound (be sure to follow all the manufacturer's product instructions). Use a figure-8 motion and work one section at a time.

5 Wipe the surface clean with a wet rag, and then use a microfiber towel to remove any lint or dust.

6 Apply the paste wax or polish by hand with a sponge or foam pad using a circular motion. After the wax forms a hazy appearance, rub it off with a soft cloth. (Be sure to follow all the manufacturer's product instructions.)

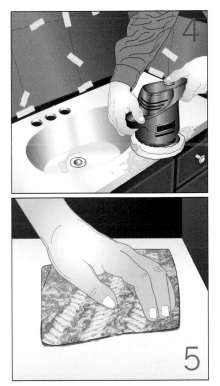

What about granite or marble countertops?

Over time, granite and marble will get fine scratches on their surface, the seal will wear away, and anything that comes in contact with them will literally absorb into the stone—including soap, cosmetic products, lotions, water, and so on.

The only way to prevent this staining and dulling is to clean them properly and keep them sealed. Here's a test—drop water on your countertop. If it doesn't bead up, it's time to apply a sealer. Find one recommended by a stone dealer (like Stone Spray-N-Seal) and follow the application directions. As for general cleaning, never use products that contain ammonia or bleach. Clean them regularly with a pH mild product like Simple Green Stone Cleaner.

But what if you already have stains or scratches? First, you must identify the cause of the stain, and then you can purchase various chemical solutions that are stain specific. Granite and marble restoration kits are also available and include various refinishing materials. After the stain is removed, the surface will need to be resealed.

It's always best to use products that are recommended by a stone professional and made specifically for your countertop material. Always follow all the manufacturer's instructions and safety precautions.

If your granite or marble countertop is in really bad shape—deep etching, dark stains—call in a professional stone-restoration company.

Hang an Adjustable Tilt Mirror

WHAT YOU'LL NEED

Tilting mirror with installation hardware

Various screwdrivers

Allen wrench (hex keys)

Drill and appropriate drill bit(s)

Blanket or towel

Tape measure

Pencil

Level

Electronic stud finder

Anchors and screws*

Washers*

* If applicable

Not only does this type of mirror add a level of elegance and charm to your bathroom or dressing area, it's also highly functional. The pivoting action allows for various viewing angles. Adjustable tilt mirrors are the perfect choice for kids and little people.

CONSIDER THIS

- To do this project, it's likely that you'll be removing an old mirror that might create some wall damage. Some type of wall patch will be required before you install your new mirror.

- Depending on the size of the mirror, I recommend installing it with a helper to assist with lifting and positioning.

- The mirror should come with installation hardware. If it does not, be sure to use anchors and screws that can support the weight of the mirror.

- Tilt mirror installations vary depending on style and brand. The following are general instructions for installing this type of mirror. Always follow the manufacturer's instructions and safety precautions.

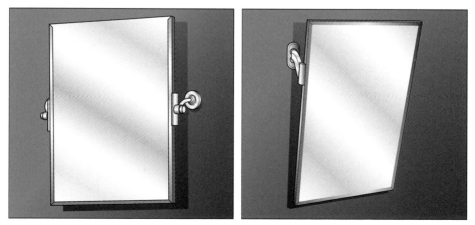

A standard adjustable tilt mirror is shown on the left. The mirror on the right is specifically designed for a person using a wheelchair.

PREP WORK

- Prepare the wall for installation. This may include removing an old mirror, patching, and painting. See "Patch Walls in Drywall" on page 52. If you're removing a large glued vanity mirror, see the sidebar "How can I safely remove a large vanity wall mirror?" on page 146.

- If working above a sink and vanity, cover it with a blanket or towel to prevent possible damage from a falling part or tool.

THE PROJECT

1 After reviewing your mirror's measurements, determine the desired location and mark the wall with a pencil. It's best to find the center of the sink (if applicable) and start from there.

2 Using the included mounting dimensions as a reference, mark your vertical and horizontal center for each mounting plate and check with a level.

3 Using a stud finder, determine whether these plates fall on a stud.

4 Mark the mounting-plate holes for one of the mirror posts with a pencil.

5 If one or more of the mounting-plate holes will be in drywall, make the appropriate-size hole for an anchor with a drill and drill bit. If one or more of the mounting-plate holes falls on a stud, no anchor will be necessary. Instead you'll need to predrill a pilot hole into the stud (one for each mounting-plate hole).

6 Screw in one mounting plate.

7 Repeat steps for installing the second mounting plate, and be sure to recheck your measurements and level.

8 Install the posts to the mirror as instructions dictate; this may involve using various washers. Be sure that the posts are installed in the proper orientation to the mirror.

9 With the posts secured to the mirror, mount the entire mirror assembly to the mounting plates with the provided screws; these may be small set-screws.

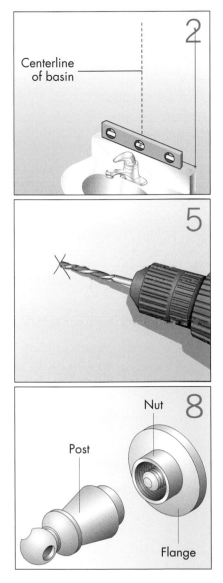

Centerline of basin

2

5

Nut

8

Post

Flange

Replace a Vanity Light Fixture

WHAT YOU'LL NEED

New light fixture with mounting hardware

Flathead and Phillips screwdrivers

Lineman pliers

Non-contact voltage tester ("pen-type" with working batteries)

Utility knife*

Mounting plate or strap*

* If applicable

The first thing I did in my new home (besides put in new door locks) was switch out the dullsville light fixtures in the bathrooms. A high-design light fixture can add a new dimension of style to your bathroom.

CONSIDER THIS

• The first rule of any electric project is to shut off the power from the service panel (breaker or fuse box). Turning the light switch to the off position does not offer enough protection. Switches are accidentally flipped on or other live wires may be in the fixture's electric box, which is why shutting off power from the service panel is crucial for your safety.

• After the power is off at the panel, be sure that no one will turn on the power as you're working.

• If you're unsure which breaker or fuse controls your bathroom fixture, here's what to do: Working with a partner, turn the light on and begin flipping breaker switches on and off as your partner monitors the light. When the light shuts off, have him yell to you. Then mark the breaker.

• With any electric project, once the power is off at the panel, recheck the box itself with an electric tester. To ensure that the tester itself is working properly, first check the power cord plugged into a live outlet and see if the tester signals electricity.

• When choosing a new fixture, make sure that it will fit in the space you have and will provide you with ample lighting. Check the maximum wattage on the new fixture you're considering.

PREP WORK

• First shut off the power to the light from the service panel.

• Removing the old fixture will vary depending on what type of light you have. Generally, you first need to remove the globe (diffuser) or light cover, and then the light bulbs.

- After you've removed the globe and bulb(s), there may be nuts that secure the fixture base to the wall. Unscrew them and pull the fixture away from the wall. If the fixture has been caulked or painted, it may help to run a utility knife around the seam where the fixture meets the wall (being careful not to damage the wall).

- Pulling out the fixture should reveal wires, an electrical box, and potentially a round mounting plate or strap. Mentally note how the wires are connected—usually black to black, white to white, ground to ground (green or copper)— because you'll need to repeat the same wiring (a).

- With an electric tester, recheck to make sure that the power is off. Hold the tester up to the wires— no light or ringing indicates no power.

- Unscrew the wire nuts and disconnect the fixture. Set the fixture aside. It's good practice to reconnect the wire nuts to the now single wires.

- If there's a mounting plate that is similar to the new one, you may leave the old. If not, remove it.

- A bare copper ground wire may be screwed to the inside of the electrical box—disconnect it.

- You should now have a black, white, and ground wire coming out of your electric box.

THE PROJECT

Installing a new fixture will vary depending on its style and brand. The following are general instructions on how to install a wall-mounted light fixture (or *sconce*). Always follow the manufacturer's instructions and safety precautions.

1 Familiarize yourself with the parts of your new fixture.

2 With the power off at the service panel, recheck the exposed wires with an electric tester to verify that the power is off.

3 Screw the mounting plate or strap onto the electrical box.

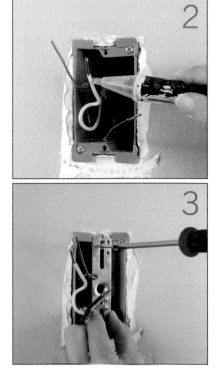

4 Rewire as your old fixture was—black to black, white to white, ground to ground or to electrical box. Be sure that your wires are properly connected and tightened with wire nuts. (If you tug on the wire nuts, you shouldn't be able to pull them off—if they come off, either screw them on tighter or use a smaller wire nuts.)

5 Carefully fold the wires into the electrical box.

6 Align the fixture over the mounting plate and, with the screws provided, secure it to the plate.

7 Screw in the light bulb(s) and then the globe. Be careful not to over-tighten the screws—doing so may crack the globe.

What if I discover my old fluorescent vanity light has no electrical box?

If you remove your old fixture and find only wires coming out from the wall with no electrical box, you must install one. Purchase a *remodel electrical box* (also known as an *old-work box* or, for a light fixture, a *round work box*). These types of boxes attach directly to the drywall, as opposed to being fastened to studs when the home is being built.

To install the electrical box, trace the box shape on the drywall where your wires come out of the wall. Cut out the shape with a drywall saw. Pull the wires through the entry holes in the back of the box. Now insert the box into the drywall hole. Secure the box to the sides of the drywall by tightening the two screws.

Be sure that your light fixture doesn't exceed the maximum weight capacity for the remodel box (usually about 10 pounds).

If the wires from your old fixture are not centered over your vanity, you'll probably need to run new wiring through studs to center the remodel box. Running new wiring is a more complex electrical project and is usually required to be performed or checked by a licensed electrician.

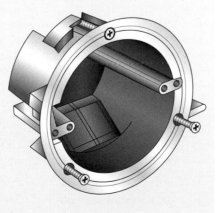

Frame a Vanity Mirror

WHAT YOU'LL NEED

Measure your mirror to determine how many lengths of molding you'll need—always buy a little extra.

Miter box or electric miter saw

Small chisel*

Utility knife*

Molding

Stain or primer and paint

Paintbrush

Blocks of wood or coffee cans

Sandpaper

Tape measure

Pencil

Clear waterproof adhesive for glass

Rags

Four corner blocks**

* If applicable

** Optional

Mirror Framing Systems

There are mirror framing systems on the market that cut out a lot of the work that comes along with building your own frame. Mirrorscapes (www.mirrorscapeframes.com) is a brand I really like because of how well they're designed and how easy they are to install. The choice of colors and styles are vast, so you're sure to find the look you want. Though a framing system may be more expensive than making your own from scratch, the payoff is ease of application and guaranteed fit and finish.

A sure way to make a simple plate-glass "builder's" mirror look like a custom showroom piece is to frame it with gorgeous molding. Suddenly that plain old mirror will become the focal point of your bathroom.

Framing a vanity mirror is also a great way to hide damaged mirror edges where the silvering behind the glass has worn away.

There are several ways to go about framing a mirror, some are more elaborate than others. The method I'm using here is very straightforward, and it accommodates any mirror placement because the molding goes directly on the mirror (as opposed to around it), allowing you to frame the mirror even if it's wall to wall across the vanity, or vanity to ceiling.

CONSIDER THIS

- Make sure you have clearance around the mirror for the addition of a frame. Something like a close medicine cabinet or towel rack could interfere with frame placement.

- Unfinished molding will need to be stained or primed and painted on the face and halfway on the underside (a ¼-inch reflection can be seen on the back of the molding) and then allowed to dry before installing.

- When choosing a molding, think about the look you'd like to create. Do you want to match the finish on the vanity? Would you prefer a metallic finish to coordinate with your fixtures? How about a chunky ornate molding to add a dramatic element to your loo? Some stores will give you sample or scrap molding to go home with to help you decide. Have fun with it! Keep in mind that large wood molding gets expensive, heavy, and challenging to cut. Medium-density fiberboard (MDF) or plastic molding is less costly, lighter, and easier to work with.

- Corner block moldings (sometimes called *rosette blocks*) are a great option to consider. They add beautiful detail and eliminate having to cut mitered corners. (See the illustration on the next page.)

PREP WORK

- Stain (if wood) or prime and paint your lengths of molding and allow for drying time. Start by first painting half the backside (that will be the inside edge to the mirror), and then flip them over and paint the face of the molding. A good way to do this is to prop up their ends on blocks of wood or coffee cans to enable you to flip them over while they're still wet, to paint the other side.

- Allow lengths and corner pieces (if applicable) to dry completely. Follow the paint or stain manufacturer's instructions and drying times.

- Note if you have metal clips that hold the mirror in place, you'll need to notch space for them using a small chisel.

THE PROJECT: Corner block moldings

Gluing the lower length first, then the sides, and then the top makes for an easier install because lengths can rest on one another while drying.

1. Dry-fit corner blocks and molding to see how they should join in relation to the lengths to the mirror. If the corner blocks are wider than the molding, mark the blocks where the lengths should be positioned to them.

2. Apply adhesive to the back of a block (follow the manufacturer's instructions and drying times). Do not put adhesive more than a ½ inch close to the inside edge. The glue will dry clear, but you still may see traces of it in the mirror's reflection. Also, allow room for the adhesive to spread as you press the block in place.

3. Press the block on the lower corner of the mirror, allowing an even overlap along the mirror edges to hide the mirror's side edge. Wipe away any excess. Glue the second block on the other side.

4. Marking materials is the best way to get an accurate measurement—take one of your molding lengths and hold it up to the glued blocks (a). With a pencil, mark the distance between the blocks. Do not use the factory edge as "one side" because it won't be square. To square the edge, mark a perpendicular line, then cut a clean squared end (b). If there are any metal hanging clips, mark their location on the molding. If you can't fit the entire length of molding in your bathroom, just take a measurement between blocks (and clips, if applicable).

5. Cut the length using your miter box. If you have clips to account for, notch out space for them along the back of the molding using a chisel. Sand smooth any cuts.

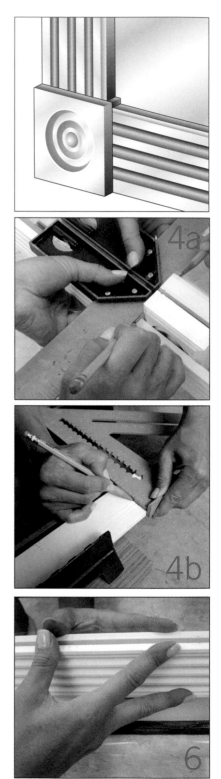

6 Dry-fit the molding. They should butt easily between the blocks. If the corner blocks are larger than your lengths, line them up to the marks you made on the blocks. Make sure the lengths sit slightly past the mirror edge—make any necessary adjustments.

7 Apply adhesive to the molding in a squiggly line and press it onto the mirror between the blocks. Remember not to apply adhesive too close to the edges. Wipe away any excess.

8 Glue the two upper corner blocks and repeat Steps 1–3.

9 Glue the sides and then the top, repeating Steps 4–7.

THE PROJECT: Mitered corners

1 Measure the length of the lower edge of the mirror and add ¼ inch to that measurement.

2 Cut a clean mitered edge on one of your molding lengths. Remember to note the top and bottom of the molding. Keep in mind that the long point of the miter cut will be the actual length of the mirror plus ⅛ inch overhang on each side (to hide the mirror's side edge).

3 With a tape measure, starting from the long point of the miter cut, mark your measurement on the molding with a pencil.

4 Using that mark as the long point of the miter cut, cut your second corner.

5 Dry-fit the lower length and make any necessary adjustments.

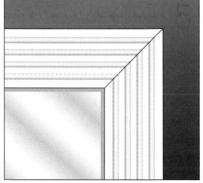

6 Apply adhesive to the molding in a squiggly line. Do not put adhesive more than ½ inch from the inside mirror edge. The adhesive will dry clear, but you still may see traces of it in the mirror's reflection. Also, allow room for adhesive to spread as you press the molding in place.

7 Press the molding onto the bottom of the mirror. Wipe away any excess.

8 Take another measurement for your two side lengths adding ⅛ inch to that measurement.

9 Follow Steps 2–7 to install the side moldings.

10 For the top molding, measure and mark the distance between the side lengths. Dry-fit it, making any adjustments. Glue, press in place, and wipe away any excess.

Showers

Don't let a shoddy showerhead ruin the joys of a great shower. Whether you're fixing a drip or updating to a handheld showerhead, the projects in this chapter will make your shower go from blah to bliss.

Replace a Showerhead

WHAT YOU'LL NEED

Replacement showerhead

Tongue-and-groove pliers (a second pair of pliers may be necessary)

Scouring pad

Teflon tape

Penetrating oil*

* If applicable

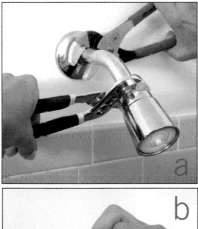

Our new home came with the most inept showerheads. Now, how is a boring little showerhead supposed to satisfy a gal who wants shower time to be an energizing romp through a waterfall, when all it gives her is a dull dance with drizzle?

There are so many exciting showerheads available today. From downpour rain heads to five-way massaging sprayers to low-flow water savers—the hardest thing about changing a showerhead is choosing one.

CONSIDER THIS

It's very important that you don't loosen the shower arm from its connection behind the wall—this could cause a leak! To ensure that you don't disrupt this connection, practice *holding back* the arm, which means holding it with your hand or pliers to prevent it from moving back as you remove or attach the showerhead.

PREP WORK

- Before removing the old showerhead, wrap the plier jaws with masking tape to avoid marring the finish.

- Holding back the shower arm with your hand (or second set of pliers if it's really tight), use your tongue-and-groove pliers to unscrew the showerhead at the nut (a). Unscrew it counterclockwise. Use penetrating oil if the showerhead won't budge.

- Remove any old Teflon tape or buildup that may be around the threads of the shower arm (b). Use a scouring pad to clean the threads.

THE PROJECT

1 Wrap new Teflon tape around the threads of the shower arm, clockwise, making two tight spins.

2 By hand, screw on the new showerhead and then snug it tight with the pliers.

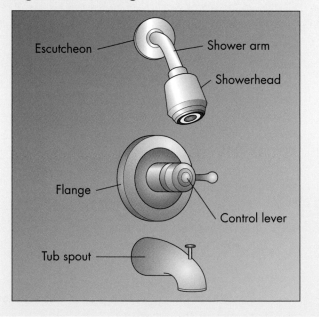

3 Turn on the water and check for leaks. Snug the showerhead on tighter if there's a leak. It may be necessary to hold back the shower arm to prevent it from spinning as you tighten the showerhead.

Replacement Shower Trim Kit

Complete tub/shower trim kits are available that can totally renew the look of your shower. A replacement trim kit is basically all the pretty stuff on the outside of the shower wall—no valves or supply pipes—just the escutcheon, showerhead, shower arm, flange, control knob (or lever) and tub spout if applicable. First identify your shower's brand and model and see if a trim kit for it is available by contacting the manufacturer or checking with a plumbing supply store.

Instructions will be included with the kit, but basically it's taking a showerhead replacement to the next level. The good news is no special plumbing skills are required. Talk about updating without remodeling!

Escutcheon — Shower arm

Showerhead

Flange

Control lever

Tub spout

Repair a Leaky Showerhead

WHAT YOU'LL NEED

Replacement cartridge

Flathead and Phillips screwdrivers

Needle-nose pliers

Tongue-and-groove pliers

Wrench*

Metal nail file or pocket knife

Cartridge puller*

Rag

Heat-resistant plumber's grease

* If applicable

If your shower is leaking from the showerhead when the water is completely shut off, you probably have a leaky cartridge or valve.

Like a leaky faucet, a shower faucet repair works the same way. You need to first identify what type of shower faucet you have. Is it a cartridge, compression, or ball type? (See "Repair a Leaky Faucet," on page 65.) The steps to repair a regular faucet can be used to repair a shower faucet with a few minor variations that you'll be able to figure out with a little hands-on inspection.

This project addresses a typical cartridge-type shower faucet.

CONSIDER THIS

To replace your faucet cartridge, you'll have to shut the water off to your shower from a shut-off valve to your bathroom or at the water main to the house.

Before attempting this project, verify that your showerhead isn't a bit clogged—if that's the case, water will build-up in the nozzle and slowly drip out when the water is shut off, mimicking a leak. (See "Clean a Showerhead," on page 26.)

If you cannot identify your shower's faucet brand and model, the best way to find a replacement is to bring the old cartridge with you to the hardware or plumbing supply store.

PREP WORK

- Shut off the water to the faucet from the shut-off valves or at the water main.
- Place a rag over the shower drain so that nothing falls down it.

THE PROJECT

1 With the water shut off from the shut-off valve or the water main, turn on the shower to check that the water is off.

2 Gently pry the decorative cap on the handle off with a metal nail file or flathead screwdriver (a). With the screw exposed, unscrew it and pull off the handle (b).

3 With the handle off, there may be a sleeve, a locking nut, and/or retaining clip(s) that need to be removed. Use a wrench or pliers to remove the sleeve or nut. Use a flathead screwdriver or needle-nose pliers to remove the clip. (Faucets vary, so you may need to work through a bit of a puzzle to remove the cap, handle, nut, clip[s] and so on, so be patient!)

4 Pull out the cartridge using pliers, but first look to see if there's a mark, flat side, or notch, and mentally note its orientation. Pulling out the cartridge may take some patience—wiggle it out little by little.

5 If the cartridge won't budge, consider using a cartridge puller, which can be purchased at a plumbing supply store (see the sidebar "Using a Cartridge Puller" below).

6 Bring the old cartridge to the store with you for the proper replacement part. Remember to note the brand of faucet. If you have a choice of brass or plastic, opt for brass—although more expensive, it lasts much longer.

7 To insert the new cartridge first recall a mark, flat side, or notch to indicate orientation. Push the new cartridge in place with your finger. The manufacturer may recommend plumber's grease.

8 Reassemble the unit—insert the retaining clip(s) locking nut, and so on (if applicable). Then reattach the handle.

9 Turn on the water from the shut-off valve or water main and test the faucet. Check to see that hot and cold water work in the proper handle position. If they're crossed (hot comes out of cold and vice versa), rotate the cartridge 180 degrees.

10 Replace the decorative cap. Finished!

Using a Cartridge Puller

When a cartridge just won't budge, which is very common with older shower faucets and in areas with hard water, you may need the assistance of a *cartridge puller.* Pullers vary according to faucet brand, so each one is set-up a little differently. Be sure to find one that is compatible with your faucet type.

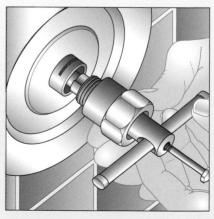

To use the puller, you insert it into or over the cartridge by pushing or screwing the puller in place. (Typically, there is a threaded screw on the puller that screws into the old valve cartridge stem.) After the puller is engaged with the old cartridge, twist the puller slightly clockwise and counterclockwise, and then pull the cartridge straight out. This will break loose any mineral buildup and set that cartridge free.

Add a Handheld Showerhead with a Slide Bar

WHAT YOU'LL NEED

Handheld showerhead with slide bar kit

Tongue-and-groove pliers (a second pair of pliers may be necessary)

Screwdriver

Nail-set (or nail punch) **and hammer**

Allen wrench (hex key)

Drill/driver

Masonry bit (see kit instructions for size)

Scouring pad

Teflon tape

Anchors and screws (should be included in kit)

Silicone caulking

Caulking gun

Penetrating oil*

* If applicable

The convenience of a height-adjustable showerhead provides a custom fit and shower experience for everyone.

Available today are handheld shower kits that connect to your existing shower arm, so installation is simple. There are also kits that offer both a fixed showerhead and a handheld showerhead that enables you to adjust back and forth between the two using a diverter switch.

CONSIDER THIS

- Take time to consider proper slide-bar placement because installation requires drilling holes in the shower wall.

- Handheld shower kits vary. These instructions below offer a typical installation. Always follow the manufacturer's instructions and safety precautions.

- If you use a silicone caulking, follow manufacturer's drying time before showering.

- Slide bars should not be used as a safety grab rail.

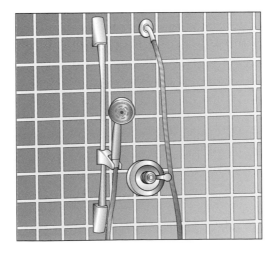

PREP WORK

- Before removing the old showerhead, wrap the plier jaws with masking tape to prevent marring the fixture finish.

- Holding back the shower arm with your hand (or second set of pliers if it's really tight), use your tongue-and-groove pliers to unscrew the showerhead at the nut (a). Unscrew it counterclockwise. Use penetrating oil if the showerhead won't budge.

- Remove any old Teflon tape or buildup that may be around the threads of the shower arm. Use a scouring pad to clean the threads.

- Wrap new Teflon tape around the threads of the shower arm, clockwise, making two tight spins (b).

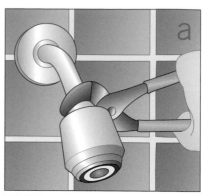

THE PROJECT

1 Determine the maximum height and right-to-left placement of the new showerhead, and then mark the wall with a pencil.

2 Using the kit's mounting bracket, mark your drill holes at the location you've chosen.

3 Measure the bar length down from the top bracket and mark the spot for the bottom bracket—use a level to make sure it's plumb (or a true vertical). Mark the drill holes. (The instructions may give a definitive length to drill the holes. If not, measure the distance of the assembled bar.)

4 Score the hole marks with a nail punch and hammer to create a starting point for the drill bit. (See the sidebar "Drilling Tips for Tile" on page 32.)

5 Drill the holes for your mounting bracket. The kit will indicate the drill bit size.

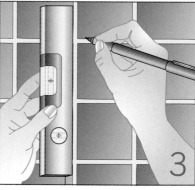

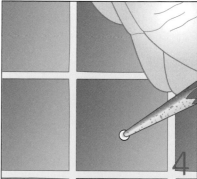

6 Insert the anchors into the holes. Put a bead of silicone caulking around the back of the mounting brackets and screw them into the anchors.

7 Assemble the slide bar. This will usually involve attaching the shower holder to the bar and a bracket cover on to each end. Make sure that the shower holder slides properly up and down the bar.

8 Put a bead of silicone caulking around the back of each bracket cover.

9 Secure the assembled bar to the mounting brackets. Typically, there will be a set-screw on each bracket cover that will screw onto the mounting brackets with an Allen wrench or screwdriver.

10 Screw the shower hose to the shower arm, and then the hand-held shower to the hose. Many kits call for hand-tightening.

11 Turn on the water to check for leaks.

12 Place your new handheld shower on the bar and admire your work. Allow the silicone to dry before using the shower.

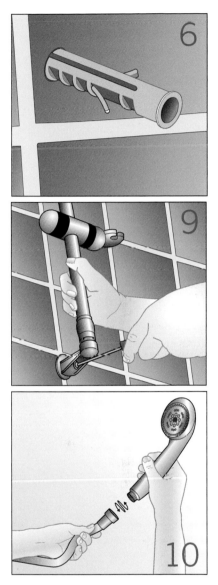

Bathtubs

Loose tiles and a faulty tub spout are all it takes to ruin an otherwise lovely bathtub. Get the fix on these projects to restore your tub into the bathing beauty it's supposed to be.

Replace a Tub Spout

WHAT YOU'LL NEED

Tub spout with correct fit (type, length, with or without diverter)

Allen wrench or screwdriver (for a slip spout)

Tongue-and-groove pliers*

Utility knife*

Teflon tape (for threaded spout)

Scouring pad (for threaded spout)

Razor scraper

Silicone caulking

Caulking gun

* If applicable

Slip spout

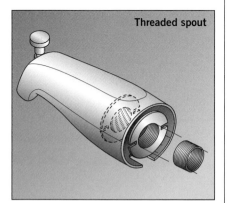

Threaded spout

Replacing a tub spout becomes more than an aesthetic update when the diverter stops working properly. It's no fun when you flip the tub spout to shower mode, but more water seeps out of the tub spout than comes out of the showerhead. That's fine if you have a fetish for exceedingly clean feet, but for trying to wash shampoo out of your hair? Not so much.

CONSIDER THIS

Getting the proper tub spout replacement is crucial, so be sure to bring the old one with you to the plumbing parts store.

PREP WORK

You'll first need to identify whether your spout is a *threaded* or a *slip* type. A slip-type spout slips over the pipe that comes from the wall (called a *nipple*) and is fastened to the nipple with a set-screw. A threaded-type spout is threaded and screws onto the nipple that protrudes from the wall.

TO REMOVE A SLIP SPOUT

- Look around under the spout, toward the wall for a slot from where the screw is accessible. With an Allen wrench or screwdriver, loosen the screw.

- Once the screw is loose, just slip off the spout. If a bead of caulking around the spout is making it difficult to unscrew, break the seal with a utility knife.

TO REMOVE A THREADED SPOUT

- By hand, and with enough force, unscrew the entire spout counterclockwise. If there is a bead of caulking around the spout making it difficult to unscrew, break the seal with a utility knife (a). You may need to use tongue-and-groove pliers if it's hard to budge (b).

- Clean off any Teflon tape or sealant from the threads with a scouring pad, and remove any caulking from the tile with a scraper (c).

THE PROJECT: Slip spout

1 Clean off any old residue on the tile with a razor scraper.

2 Slip it over the nipple and tighten the set-screw.

3 Apply a small bead of silicone caulking around the back end of the spout to create a watertight seal around the wall.

Threaded spout

THE PROJECT: Threaded spout

1 Wrap new Teflon tape clockwise around the threads of the nipple— three tight spins.

2 Screw on the new spout.

3 Apply a small bead of silicone caulking around the back end of the spout to create a watertight seal around the wall.

Replace a Damaged Tile Section

WHAT YOU'LL NEED

Replacement tiles (if the old tiles can't be reused)

Drill/driver

Hole-saw bit*

Small pry bar

Scraper

Utility knife

Drywall saw

Clean rags

Large towel or tarp

Gloves and safety glasses

Vacuum

Tape measure

Pencil

Cement board

T-square

Straightedge (or use T-square)

Cement board carbide-tipped cutter

Construction adhesive

Cement board screws

⅜-inch trowel

Thin-set mortar (latex modified)

Disposable bucket

Tile spacers

Grout

Grout float

Large man-made tile sponge

Bucket

Antifungal cleaner*

Furring strips*

* If applicable

If water seeps behind your tiles, eventually mold will grow, the wallboard will weaken, and the tiles will loosen and ultimately fall out. This is very common around tub spouts that aren't sealed properly.

CONSIDER THIS

This project will require 2 to 3 days to account for work and drying times.

PREP WORK

If your damaged section of tiles is around any fixtures, you must first remove the fixtures to get them out of the way for the new wall section and tile (see "Replace a Tub Spout" on page 91).

TO REMOVE THE OLD TILES

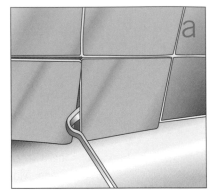

- Plug the drain with a rag and cover the basin with a towel or tarp.

- Pry out the loose tiles with a small pry bar or scraper. Firmly but carefully insert the tip of the pry bar in the loose section of the joint, and then slowly pry the tiles away from the wall (a). You can try to reuse the tiles, but you must work very carefully when you remove the tiles. Chances are, you'll need to buy replacement tiles.

- After the first course is removed, it'll be easier to slide a scraper behind the next course of tile. Wedge the scraper far enough inward to get good leverage for easier prying.

- Continue removing courses of tile until you reach a course that is firmly adhered. Tapping on the tile is a good way to tell if it's solidly attached—a hollow-sounding tile means that it's loose. Be sure to see that an undamaged section of wall is eventually revealed; this will be necessary to attach the new section of wall.

- If you're reusing tile, use the scraper to remove adhesive from the tile.

TO REMOVE THE OLD WALL SECTION

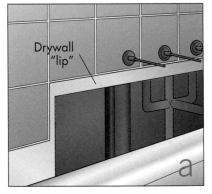

Drywall "lip"

- With a utility knife and straightedge score the length of wall that needs to be removed. Doing so will diminish the chances of disturbing the rest of the wall when removing the damaged section. Leave a perimeter or "lip" of undamaged wall; you'll butt up to that when fastening the new cement board.

- Use a drywall saw to cut out the damaged wall section going through the lengths you've scored. Remove any nails or screws that are securing the damaged wall to the studs. Pull out the damaged wall section (a).

- Be sure that the framing is sound. (If you find the wood is wet, soft, and rotted, you'll need to remove a larger section of tile and wall, and then reinforce the framing with new wood. At this point, you may consider bringing in a professional.)

- If mold has grown on the framing, wipe down the studs with an antifungal cleaner.

- Wipe away any remaining debris and vacuum the entire area so you don't damage your tub surface by grinding debris into it.

- Allow the entire area to dry out completely before continuing this project.

THE PROJECT: Replacing a wall section

1 Measure the opening in the wall.

2 Transfer the measurement of the opening to the cement board and cut it to size (see the sidebar "Cutting Cement Board" on page 96).

3 Test-fit the cement board in the opening. You shouldn't have to force the board in place. Make sure the new board sits flush with the existing wall; you may need to build out the studs with furring strips if the board sits too low.

4 When you're sure of a proper fit, apply construction adhesive to the studs and press the board in place.

5 Using cement board screws, fasten the board to the studs.

THE PROJECT: Reinstalling tile

6 Mix the thin-set mortar according to the manufacturer's directions.

7 Using a ⅜-inch trowel, apply the thin-set to a section of cement board—spread enough for a two or three tiles.

8 Press each new tile in place, making sure they sit flush with the existing tiles and with one another. Use the butt of your fist to gently pound the tile against the wall to be sure they make solid contact with the thin-set. If applicable, use appropriate-size tile spacers for accurate grout lines, or for a small section, you can space them by eye. For a bottom course of tiles that run along the tub, be sure to create a joint for the grout line with spacers—don't let them sit right on the tub.

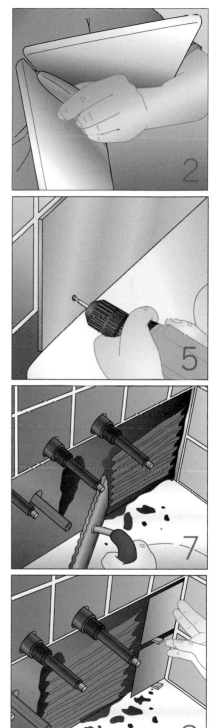

9 With a scraper, clean out any thin-set mortar that may have oozed out of the joints. Wipe away any mortar that may have gotten on the face of the tiles. Allow 24 hours for tiles to set before grouting.

10 To fill in grout lines, use a grout float to press the grout into the joints of the tile lines. It's best to hold the float at an angle and pass over the area firmly in a diagonal direction.

11 With a damp sponge, gently wipe away the grout that remains on the face of the tile.

12 As the grout dries, a powdery residue will form. Gently wipe away the residue with a soft, clean rag, being careful not to wipe out any of the grout. Let the grout dry overnight.

13 Replace any fixtures that you've removed.

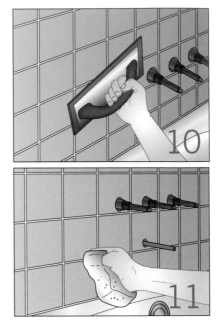

Cutting Cement Board

Cement board (a.k.a. WonderBoard or backer board) is the only choice for wet areas like tubs and showers. Cutting it can be tough if you don't have the right tool. I find the easiest way to cut cement board is with a special knife. A good carbide-tipped cement board cutter is my choice over a circular saw or jigsaw. While a hand tool will require more elbow grease, I prefer it to the mess of dust that a power tool makes.

To cut the cement board, first transfer the measurement of your opening onto the board using a T-square. On the inside of the cut line, use the cutter tool to score your mark, making several passes with the help of a straightedge to help keep your line straight. Be sure to penetrate the mesh. Then apply pressure to the back of the cement board and firmly snap the scored piece back at the scored line. Once it "cracks" open at the scored line, use a utility knife from the backside to finish cutting through the board.

It's important to be accurate with your measurements and cuts. When cutting, it's typically recommended to err on the larger side, knowing that you can trim something down. However, unlike wood or drywall, cement board is not a friendly material when it comes to shaving off small amounts.

If you need to cut a hole for a pipe fixture, transfer the placement measurement onto the cement board and use a drill with an appropriate-size hole-saw bit to make the opening.

Toilets

All the mysteries of your toilet, like that "ghost flush" and incessant running, are revealed and vanquished in this chapter. You'll also learn how to clear a stubborn clog when plunging just won't do the trick.

Unclog a Toilet with an Auger

WHAT YOU'LL NEED

Closet auger

Rubber gloves**

Safety glasses*

Mask*

Bucket

Disinfectant cleaner

* If applicable

** Optional

When a plunger just isn't doing the trick, it's time to get serious with a closet auger. This type of *plumber's snake* (see the sidebar "Snake Through Tough Clogs" on the next page) is specially designed with a shape that conforms to a toilet and plastic sheathing that won't scratch the bowl's porcelain surface.

PREP WORK

- **Warning:** If you have attempted to use a commercial drain cleaner to clear a clog prior to using an auger, you must take safety precautions. Wear safety glasses, gloves, and a mask to protect yourself from the harsh chemicals that may splash on you during the auger process.

- Turn off the water at the toilet shut-off valve.

- If the toilet is filled to the rim, wait a little while to let it drain down before starting to snake it. If the bowl is completely filled and stagnant, you may want to use a small bucket to scoop out some of the water and . . . stuff. I know this seems utterly vile, but better to have the muck contained in a bucket than splashing around the bathroom as you try to maneuver the snake through it.

- Lift up the toilet seat.

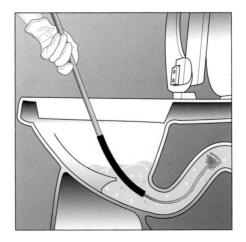

THE PROJECT

1 Feed the corkscrew tip of the auger down into the toilet and begin pressing and turning the handle clockwise, until the curved plastic sheathing is resting at the mouth of the drain.

2 Continue turning the handle firmly as the coil works its way through the clog. When the clog begins to break up, the water in the bowl will begin draining.

3 Once you're through the clog, slowly pull out the auger.

4 Dump a full bucket of water down the toilet to clear away the debris.

5 Turn on the water valve and give the toilet a flush. If it's still clogged, repeat these steps.

6 Rinse the auger with a disinfectant cleaner and let it dry before putting it away.

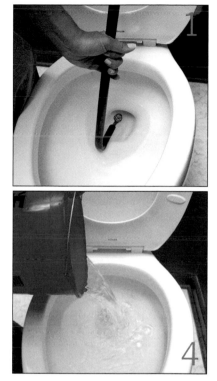

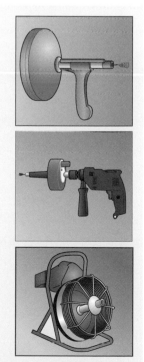

Snake Through Tough Clogs

Plumber's snakes (a.k.a. drain or trap snake, drum auger, toilet jack, and so on) are flexible augers that can be used to get through a variety of clogs in a variety of ways. For example, they can be used through a clean-out of a sink drain or down the overflow of a tub drain. They also come in various sizes and types. Small manual snakes are very effective, but for tougher clogs you can find handheld drill-driven ones. Just be careful when using this type—they have a tendency to whip around, especially as you pull them out.

Larger motorized snakes are available for rent, but I don't recommend them for novices. These units are very powerful and could potentially damage pipes or, worse yet, you! Leave these tools for the professionals. Don't let this discourage you—barring some radical exceptions, practically no drain clog is safe from the fierce bite of a nonmotorized plumber's snake.

⊙DVD Replace a Flapper

WHAT YOU'LL NEED

Replacement flapper

Old towel

Bucket

Large man-made sponge

Scrubber pad, fine sandpaper, or steel wool

If you hear your toilet running or suddenly refilling itself ("ghost" flushing), the first thing you should check is the flapper. A faulty flapper is an extremely common problem that causes toilets to waste thousands of gallons of water a year.

A toilet flapper (or stopper) is part of the flush valve assembly in the tank that opens and closes, allowing water to pass from the tank to the bowl when you flush the toilet. If a flapper is worn or misaligned, it no longer seals the flush valve (valve seat) and will cause the toilet to keep refilling itself as the water level drops in the tank.

To do a quick check on the flapper's condition, just roll up your sleeve, stick your hand in the toilet tank, and run your fingers around the flapper— chances are black rubber will get all over your fingers, indicating that it's degraded and failing.

CONSIDER THIS

Toilet flappers vary as to how they attach in the tank. It's always best to bring the old part with you to the store for a replacement. You may find an exact replacement or universal-fit flapper. I highly recommend replacing the old flapper with one that's made of silicone-coated rubber and has a no-kink, no-rust chain, like the Hornet flapper. It won't degrade over time the way a rubber flapper would, and it'll last far longer than other flappers, especially in areas where hard water is an issue.

PREP WORK

- Before emptying the tank, turn off the water to the toilet at the shut-off valve, or at the water main if one isn't designated to that toilet.

- Remove the lid and place it on a folded towel out of the way.

- Flush the toilet a couple of times.

- With a large sponge, soak up any remaining water in the tank. Squeeze out the sponge into a bucket and repeat until the tank is water free (a).

THE PROJECT

1 Unhook the chain or unscrew the lift wire from the flush lever.

2 Pull off the flapper from the overflow tube. It may be hooked in place with "wings" on either side of it, or have a large thick ring that will be pulled up and over the overflow tube.

3 Clean the tank outlet (flush valve) with a scrubber pad or steel wool to remove any mineral buildup. The valve should be smooth, not pitted, in order for it to seal properly. If there are cracks in the valve seat, it must be replaced (see "Replace a Flush Valve" on page 104).

4 To install the new flapper, first make any modifications to the replacement flapper as recommended by the manufacturer (if it's not an exact replacement).

5 Attach the flapper to the overflow tube making sure that it drops directly over the valve seat. Raise and lower the stopper to make sure it's attached properly.

6 Attach the chain or lift wire to the flush lever.

7 Trip the flush lever to see if the chain or wire is in the proper position or length. With the flapper in the closed-down position, the chain should neither be taut nor have too much slack. Be aware that the flush lever should not hit the tank lid when flushing; if it does, shorten the chain and remove excess chain links.

8 Turn on the water, let the tank fill, and give it a test flush.

Repair a Leaky Flush Valve

WHAT YOU'LL NEED

Flush valve seat repair kit (sealant ring, flapper unit, and chain)

Bucket

Large man-made sponge

Fine sandpaper

Rag

Blow dryer

A flush valve controls the passing of water from the tank to the bowl when you flush. If your toilet flush valve (valve seat) is damaged—pitted and cracked—it won't create a seal with the flapper, even if the flapper is brand new. Repairing the valve with a new seat is necessary when scrubbing the old one doesn't correct the problem. Luckily, flush valve seat repair kits are available that can quickly and easily resurface the seat without having to replace the entire flush valve assembly.

CONSIDER THIS

Flush valve seat repair kits vary, and not all toilets can use them. Note your toilet brand and take a picture of your flush valve to seek out a kit.

The following instructions describe a common repair kit application. It's always best to read the manufacturer's instructions and safety precautions.

PREP WORK

- Before emptying the tank, turn off the water to the toilet at the shut-off valve, or at the water main if one isn't designated for that toilet.

- Remove the lid and store it on a folded towel out of the way.

- Flush the toilet a couple of times.

- With a large sponge, soak up any remaining water in the tank. Squeeze out the sponge into a bucket and repeat until the tank is water free.

THE PROJECT

1 Disconnect the chain or lift wire from the flush lever and remove the old flapper.

2 Sand the valve seat until it's as smooth as possible.

3 Wipe away any debris with a clean, wet rag.

4 Thoroughly dry the valve seat—this step is crucial for proper adhesion of the new sealant ring. Use a blow dryer to help get it completely dry.

5 Peel the paper off one side of the sealant ring and press it lightly down onto the drain seat opening. Don't remove the paper from the other side yet.

6 Examine where to position the flapper unit. Test-fit it in different positions, finding the best orientation that allows the flapper to open and close without any interference with other parts (including the chain).

7 With the proper orientation established, peel off the remaining paper from the sealant ring and firmly press the flapper unit over the drain seat.

8 Attach the chain to the flush lever. Trip the flush lever to see if the chain is in the proper position and length. With the flapper in the closed-down position, the chain should neither be taut nor have too much slack. The flush lever shouldn't hit the tank lid when flushing; if it does, shorten the chain and remove excess chain links.

9 Turn on the water, let the tank fill, and give it a test flush.

If it ain't broke, don't fix it! Or should you?

I live by this rule. Why open up a can of worms for myself if I don't have to? This rule is especially true in plumbing. When you disturb seals that have been there for a while—minding their own business, holding up perfectly fine—chances are, when you tighten them back up, they're going to leak. This could mean having to replace shut-off valves, supply lines, gaskets, washers, and so on—when you never really had to. So why not repair a flush valve instead of replacing one if that does the trick?

However, there are instances when the risk of something failing can be so damaging or troublesome to correct that it's well worth fixing *before* it breaks. Here are some examples:

- Old vinyl supply lines are susceptible to bursting—replace them with braided stainless-steel ones.
- Slight drip or signs of corrosion around old shut-off valves. Replace them with ¼-turn shut-offs. (See "Replace a Shut-off Valve," on page 168.)
- A leaky washer in your faucet or toilet. Go ahead and replace all the washers, gaskets, and/or O-rings. You're already in there.

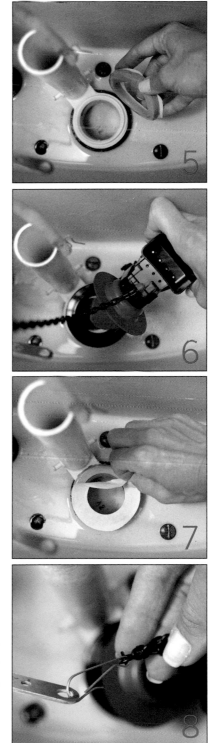

Replace a Flush Valve

WHAT YOU'LL NEED

Flush valve replacement

Flathead or Phillips screwdriver

Tongue-and-groove pliers

Pipe wrench

Bucket

Rug or cardboard

Large man-made sponge

Large towel

New supply line washer or a new stainless-steel braided supply line (if the existing one is vinyl)

New tank-to-bowl gasket

New tank-to-bowl bolt kit

Rag

Penetrating oil*

Hacksaw*

Flashlight*

* If applicable

If the entire flush valve unit is old, worn, and no longer functioning properly, you'll have a variety of symptoms like constant running, "ghost" flushing, and even a leak from the bottom of the tank. At this point, it's probably best to replace the entire flush valve unit.

CONSIDER THIS

- To find a flush valve replacement, note your toilet brand and take a picture of the old one.

- For this project, you'll need to lift the tank from the bowl, which may be heavy for one person.

- Because you'll be disconnecting the water supply line to the tank, disrupting that seal may perpetuate a small leak when it's reattached. For this reason, I recommend replacing the washer in the supply line. Or, if it's an old vinyl supply, replace it with a new flexible braided stainless-steel one. To avoid other leaks, it's best to replace the tank-to-bowl gasket, bolts, washers, and nuts. Bring the old parts to the plumbing store for proper replacements.

- The following instructions describe a common flush valve replacement. It's always best to read the manufacturer's instructions and safety precautions.

PREP WORK

- Before emptying the tank, turn off the water to the toilet at the shut-off valve, or at the water main if one is not designated to that toilet.

- Remove the lid and store it on a folded towel out of the way.

- Flush the toilet a couple of times.

- With a large sponge, soak up any remaining water in the tank. Squeeze out the sponge into a bucket and repeat until the tank is water free.

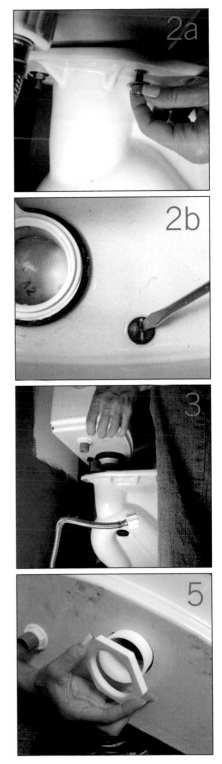

THE PROJECT

REMOVE THE OLD FLUSH VALVE UNIT

1 Disconnect the water supply line from the tank by unscrewing it by hand or with tongue-and-groove pliers.

2 Unbolt the tank from the bowl by unscrewing the nuts from beneath the tank (a). Pull out the bolts and washers from inside the tank (b). If they're rusty and stuck, spray some penetrating oil to help loosen them.

3 Pull the tank up off the bowl. Be careful to brace yourself when lifting because the tank may be heavy. (You may want to work with a partner when lifting if you're not feeling Herculean.) Place it upside down on a rug or cardboard to protect it while working.

4 Pry off the old rubber gasket. Rubber gaskets are usually one round ring, but they may sometimes be more elaborate. You may contact the toilet manufacturer for an exact replacement, but any "universal" tank-to-bowl rubber gasket replacement should do the trick. It will likely be a black ugly mess because of the corroded rubber and such, and it'll surely get all over your hands. Wipe away any debris.

5 Unscrew the large locknut that secures the flush valve to the tank. Use penetrating oil if it won't budge. Don't force it—this could crack the tank. Hold back on the flush valve from inside the tank to prevent it from spinning as you unscrew it from underneath.

6 Disconnect the refill tube from the overflow pipe and unhook the chain from the old flapper.

7 Pull out the old flush valve unit.

Is water leaking from under your tank?

Sometimes the "guts" (flush valve, fill valve) of your tank will be in perfect working order and yet you find water dripping from behind or under your tank. If this is the case, there's a seal failing somewhere—the supply line, tank-to-bowl gasket, or mounting bolts. To fix a tank leak, refer to the project above, which includes all these various part replacements.

INSTALL THE NEW FLUSH VALVE UNIT

8 Insert the new flush valve in the hole and examine its height. The overflow pipe needs to be 1 inch lower than the hole in the tank for the flush lever. This is critical to avoid a flood. Also, it should be 1 inch below the "Critical Level" (C.L.) of the fill valve. Use a hacksaw to cut the pipe if necessary.

9 With the proper overflow pipe height established, install the new flush valve by inserting it in the holes. Hand-tighten the locknut, and then give it a half-turn with your wrench or pliers. Do not over-tighten.

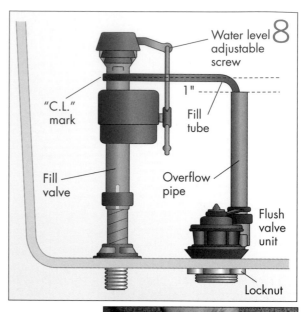

10 Slide the tank-to-bowl gasket on to the bottom of the flush valve.

11 Place the bolts (with fiber washers attached) into the mounting holes.

12 Place the tank over the bowl, guiding the bolts into the mounting holes.

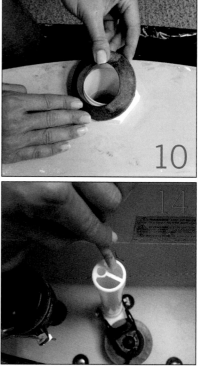

13 Place the washers and nuts onto the bolts and tighten them. Do not spin the bolts themselves—this will break the seal they create with the fiber washer. Tighten them down from the nuts, a little bit at a time on each side, so that the tank sits level when it's fully bolted in place. Again, do not over-tighten the bolts, or the tank could crack. The tank should sit solidly on the bowl when it's fully tightened. Give the tank a little shake to check.

14 Reconnect the fill tube to the overflow pipe. Don't put it directly into the pipe (this could cause the tube to siphon water); put it just above the pipe. There may be a special clip for this attachment. Aim the tube so the water hits the wall on the inside of the tube.

15 Attach the chain to the flush lever. Trip the flush lever to see if the chain is in the proper position and length. With the flapper in the closed-down position, the chain should neither be taut nor have too much slack. Be aware that the flush lever shouldn't hit the tank lid when flushing—if it does, shorten the chain and remove excess chain links.

16 Connect the new supply line without over-tightening. Turn on the water and check for leaks. Use a flashlight to help get a better look.

17 Flush the bowl and check for leaks at the tank-to-bowl seal. Now check that the whole flushing action is operating properly.

Replace a Fill Valve (or Float Cup)

WHAT YOU'LL NEED

Fill valve replacement

Tongue-and-groove pliers

New supply line washer or new braided stainless-steel supply line (if the existing one is vinyl)

Bucket

Large man-made sponge

Towel

Scrubber pad

Penetrating oil*

Utility scissors*

* If applicable

A *fill valve* (a.k.a. tank valve or ball cock when it has a ball float) fills your tank with water when you flush and shuts the water off when it reaches a certain level. A float cup or ball is used to detect the water level and will engage or disengage the fill valve—that is, if it's working properly.

If your tank fills slowly, or the water runs continuously, it's probably a faulty fill valve.

CONSIDER THIS

- Before replacing the fill valve, try fine-tuning the tank water level by bending the float arm downward, turning the brass screw, or adjusting the water level mechanism on your fill valve. This may correct the problem.

- If your tank has a rubber float, check to make sure that it isn't waterlogged. This could engage the fill valve when it shouldn't and mislead you into thinking your fill valve is defective. Unscrew it from the float arm to check its condition. Replace it with a plastic one if necessary.

- To find a fill valve replacement, note your toilet brand and take a picture of the old one.

- The following instructions describe a common float cup-type fill valve replacement. It's always best to read the manufacturer's instructions and safety precautions.

PREP WORK

- Before emptying the tank, turn off the water to the toilet at the shut-off valve, or at the water main if a valve is not designated to that toilet.

- Remove the lid and store it on a folded towel out of the way.

- Flush the toilet a couple of times.

- With a large sponge, soak up any remaining water in the tank. Squeeze out the sponge into a bucket and repeat until the tank is water free.

THE PROJECT

REMOVE THE OLD FILL VALVE

1 Disconnect the water supply line from the tank.

2 Beneath the tank unscrew the nut that secures the fill valve to the tank. Spray it with penetrating oil if it won't budge.

3 Unhook the fill tube from the overflow pipe.

4 Pull out the old fill valve, and keep it for reference.

5 Clean the area around the hole with a scrubber pad, and remove any debris.

INSTALL THE NEW FILL VALVE

6 Examine the height of the old fill valve and adjust the new one to match it exactly. There should be a spinning part that allows you to adjust its height. Note the "Critical Level" (C.L.) mark on the fill valve. Use this as reference when you're matching the height of the new one.

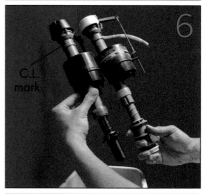

7 Place the gasket around the hole at the bottom of the tank, and then insert the fill valve into the hole. Make sure this gasket fits properly—this is what prevents the water from leaking out of the tank.

8 Orient it so the fill tube nipple is aimed at the overflow tube. Be sure that any moving components in the tank can move freely.

9 Slip the washer and nut to the bottom of the fill valve beneath the tank, and tighten it by hand. Push down on the valve shank while tightening from beneath—do not over-tighten.

10 Attach the new fill tube to the nipple on the fill valve. Now attach the other end tube to the overflow pipe. Do not put it directly into the pipe (this could cause the tube to siphon water); put it just above the pipe. There may be a special clip for this attachment. Aim the tube so the water hits the wall on the inside of the tube. Trim the fill tube if it's too long.

11 Reattach the supply line.

12 Turn the water on at the shut-off valve and check for leaks.

13 Using a screwdriver, set the water level adjustment mechanism on the float cup so the water rises to proper tank level (approximately ¾ inch lower than the overflow pipe).

14 Give it a test flush.

Honor Thy "Stemmie"

What the devil is a *Stemmie,* you ask? It's insider plumbing lingo for a person who is all-knowing, a master, a guru—simply put, a plumbing *god.* All the trades have their version of a Stemmie. If you're lucky enough to meet one, don't take it for granted—they're gems, I tell you! Once you get past their sometimes gruff exterior, they're more than eager to share their expertise with you. They have a wealth of knowledge—especially with the materials used in homes in your neighborhood for decades—that only time and experience can bring. You just can't get that from a book!

A Stemmie is often the grizzled-haired guy behind the counter of a parts shop. At a glance he can rattle off the brand, make, model number, features, benefits, and drawbacks of just about any old part you drop on his counter. I've learned so much from these guys—cousin Sal, Joe Barry, John, Wes, and, of course, the nationally renowned Bill "Stemmie" Harper. I've picked their brains about the how's and why's—hanging on every word.

So if you come across a Stemmie, I urge you to show him some love! Bring him a cup of coffee, give him a charming smile, tell him a racy joke. Trust me—when you're pulling your hair out because you can't figure out why that part you got from the home center won't thread right, you'll be so happy you did.

Walls and Floors

Safety comes first, especially in a bathroom. Also high on the priority list is extra storage and comfort. Explore the projects in this chapter to make your bathroom the safe, comfy, and convenient space you want it to be.

Install Grab Bars or Hand Grips

WHAT YOU'LL NEED

Grab bar or hand grip

Flathead or Phillips screwdriver

Nail-set (or nail punch) **and hammer**

Drill driver

Masonry bit (slightly larger than mounting screws)

Wood bit (slightly smaller than mounting screws)

Newspaper or towel

Rag

Electronic stud finder

Level

1½-inch masking tape

Safety glasses

Pencil or grease pencil

Fine-point marker

Silicone caulking

Caulking gun

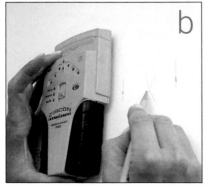

Here's an alarming statistic: Falls are the number one cause of injury and accidental death around the home. It seems to me, grab bars should be more than the right choice for people with disabilities and seniors, especially when so many beautiful designs, finishes, and colors are available today.

CONSIDER THIS

- Take your time selecting your grab bar and its placement (a). Will a child be using it in the bathtub? Is it at the right position to help you stand up from the tub? Consider all of the scenarios in which it would be used, in order to choose the right length and placement.

- Know that mounting it at a 45-degree angle, as opposed to horizontally, will accommodate people of various heights.

- Know that *both* ends of a grab bar *must* be mounted into studs.

- Look for a grab bar with a mounting flange that has adjustable screw openings to ensure proper attachment to the stud fastening, like on the Moen SecureMount Grab Bar.

- For help with drilling into tile, see the sidebar "Drilling Tips for Tile" on page 32.

- Grab bars mount differently depending on the brand. It's always best to follow manufacturer's instructions and safety precautions.

PREP WORK

- Protect the area beneath where you'll be drilling with a towel or newspaper.

- Use a stud finder to locate the studs in the area where you want to mount the grab bar (b). Mark them with a pencil or grease pencil, if on tile. For help locating the stud center, see the "How do I find the center of a stud?" sidebar on page 112.

- With a level, place a strip of masking tape down the wall to indicate the stud locations.

THE PROJECT

1 Take the grab bar and position the ends over the masking tape indicating the studs. Remember *both* ends *must* be mounted solidly into studs. If mounting horizontally or vertically, check for level or plumb.

2 If the bar has a decorative cover to conceal the screws, slide it out of the way to expose the mounting flange. Holding the bar in place with a fine-point marker, mark the three screw holes to be drilled on each end.

3 Before drilling your pilot hole, use masking tape or etch the tile mark with a nail-set to prevent the drill bit from walking.

4 Drill your pilot hole with a masonry bit. When you're through the tile, be sure you hit wood, and stop drilling. Switch to your wood bit and drill your pilot holes into the studs. Wipe away any debris.

5 Insert a little silicone into each hole (a) and then on the backs of the grab bar ends (b).

6 Place your grab bar ends over the pilot holes (sliding any decorative cover well out of the way). With the mounting flange lined up with your holes, thread any washers onto the wood screws and drive the screws through the flange into the holes. Wipe away any silicone that may have oozed out. **Note:** Setups will vary, but you will likely need to screw in one flange first, and then insert the bar and second flange. Screw the second flange into the wall.

7 Slide on any decorative cover over the mounting flange—spin/ snap it in place. Don't wet the area until the silicone has dried. See manufacturer's instructions for drying times.

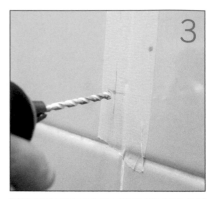

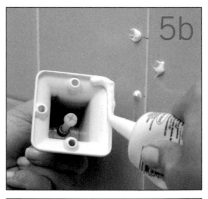

How do I find the center of a stud?

For a secure installation into a stud, you have to be sure all the screws are driving into a meaty part of the wood. A screw mounted just at the edge of a stud can easily break away with enough weight or force, especially dangerous when using a grab bar.

To find the stud center, slide your stud finder in one direction along the wall; as soon as it beeps, make a mark. This should be one edge of the stud. Then come from the other direction and do the same. This will be the other edge of the stud. The space in between your two marks will be the stud center—the most secure spot for screw placement.

Hang an Over-the-Toilet Cabinet

WHAT YOU'LL NEED

Over-the-toilet cabinet

Screwdriver

Drill/driver

Drill bits for pilot holes

Newspaper or towel

Mounting hardware (wood screws, toggle bolts)

24-inch level

Pencil

Tape measure

It seems there's never enough storage space in a bathroom, especially for gals who love their bath-and-body products. I admit it—I'm one of them. I presently have more lotions, creams, cleansers, and exfoliators in one cabinet than any person should own in a lifetime. This especially upsets my husband when he reaches for a roll of toilet paper but comes out with a roll of waxing strips.

A great place to reclaim storage space is over the toilet. With a variety of cabinet styles available these days, you'll be adding an attractive element of design to your bathroom as well.

CONSIDER THIS

• It's best to secure a cabinet to at least one stud. Even if the cabinet is small, products in it will soon increase its load, and anchors alone may not give the proper support.

• It's easier to do this project with a partner who can help you lift and secure the cabinet over the toilet.

PREP WORK

• Protect the toilet with a large towel or blanket.

• With a stud finder, locate the studs behind your toilet; use a level to mark their location. Chances are that only one stud may fall at the chosen location to mount your cabinet.

THE PROJECT

1 Position the cabinet over the toilet—center it and raise it to your preferred height. Mark its locations on the wall with a pencil and level on the left, right, top, and bottom sides. These lines will be crucial for installation, so make sure to use a level on the cabinet.

2 On the wall, take a measurement of the distance of the side of the cabinet to the stud using the marks you've made.

3 Take that measurement and transfer it to the back of the cabinet; use a level to mark it. Now you know where to drill the holes that will correspond with the stud.

4 Knowing where the stud holes will be made, mark another set of holes on the cabinet's other side. These holes will take toggle bolts (assuming that the side doesn't hit a stud).

5 With a wood bit, drill the marked holes through the back of the cabinet. For the holes that take toggle bolts, use a drill bit large enough to fit the bolt.

6 Raise the cabinet over the toilet and put it in position (using the marks you've made to line it up on the wall). Through the holes you just made in the cabinet, mark the wall with a pencil.

7 With the screw holes now marked, drill pilot holes through the drywall into the stud. Next, drill holes through the drywall for the toggle bolts (assuming that the side doesn't hit a stud). Make the hole large enough so the wings can slip through them.

8 Insert the bolts into the holes of the cabinet you've made for the toggle bolts, and then thread the wings from behind (making sure that the wings are facing the right direction). See also the sidebar "Toggle Bolt—Next Best Thing to a Stud" on the next page.

9 Raise the cabinet and inset the wings of the toggle into the holes on the wall you made. Tighten the toggle bolt by driving the screws from inside the cabinet. (To engage the wings against the back of the wall, pull back on the bolt as you're driving it.) Check for level before tightening completely.

10 Drive the wood screws on the other side of the cabinet straight into the studs.

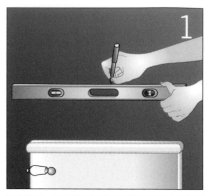

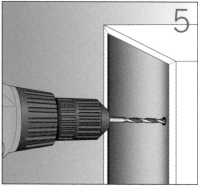

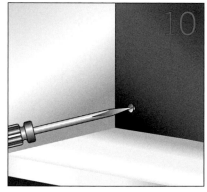

Toggle Bolt—Next Best Thing to a Stud

When you want to mount something heavy on a wall or ceiling, the most secure way to do so is to screw right into a stud or joist. But what do you do if that framing member isn't where you need it (which almost always ends up being the case)? Ugh.

A whole host of drywall anchors are out there, but for heavy-duty applications, a spring-loaded toggle bolt is the way to go. When you insert the toggle through the wall, wings open up and apply pressure against the back of the wall as you tighten the bolt.

But here's the thing you have to be aware of, in order to use a toggle bolt, you have to make a hole big enough through the wall (and sometimes whatever it is you're hanging) to slip the wings through. Now what do you do with this big hole? You have two solutions: Either thread a washer behind the head of the bolt to account for that hole or insert the bolt through the front of the object you're hanging, and then thread the wings from behind it. Just be sure the wings face the right direction so when they pop open, the tips hit the wall.

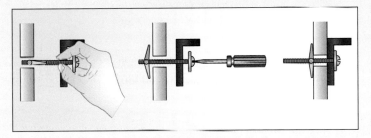

Install a GFCI

WHAT YOU'LL NEED

GFCI outlet and plate cover

Flathead or Phillips screwdriver

Small jeweler's-type screwdriver*

Non-contact voltage tester ("pen-type" with working batteries)

Electrical tape

Masking tape*

* if applicable

A GFCI or GFI (ground fault circuit interrupter) is basically an outlet designed with a built-in circuit breaker of sorts. It monitors the flow of electrical current in a circuit. If there's an electrical leak (ground fault), it senses the variance of current and will shut itself off in a fraction of a second, which could save your life. If your home is old and/or the outlets in damp areas (especially in bathrooms) have not been updated with GFCIs, you should definitely replace them.

CONSIDER THIS

- Depending on your outlet, you may need to work with live electrical wires.

- Before starting this project, find out which circuit breaker or fuse controls the outlet you want to replace.

PREP WORK

TO TEST THE OUTLET

- Shut the power from the service panel to the outlet.

- Test the outlet with a non-contact voltage tester to be sure the power is off (a).

TO REMOVE THE OLD OUTLET

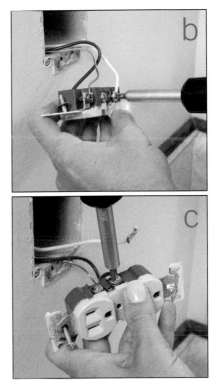

- With the power off, unscrew the cover plate.

- Unscrew the metal ears of the outlet and pull it out.

- Unscrew the wires from the terminals—black, white, and ground (green or bare copper). If the wires are "back wired," use a jeweler's flat screwdriver to depress the tab next to each wire hole and pull out the wire (b and c).

- Straighten the curve on the wires and cap each black wire and white wire with a wire nut.

   If your outlet has two wires (plus a ground), continue to Step 1.

   If your outlet has four wires (plus two grounds), it's part of a branch circuit.

- Determine which is the *incoming* set of black/white wires carrying current from and back to the service panel. To make this distinction, you'll need to work with the power *on*. **Warning:** Do not let the live wire tips touch anything but the wire nuts. It's safe to handle the wires by the plastic sheathing.

- With each wire separated and capped, turn the power *on* at the service panel. *You will be working with live wires.*

- Test which wires are incoming (live). Test one black wire at a time with the pen-type non-contact voltage tester.

- After you've identified which black/white set of wires is from the service panel, wrap a small tab of masking tape around them so you remember which ones they are.

THE PROJECT

A GFCI is labeled LINE and LOAD.

IF YOUR OUTLET HAS TWO WIRES (PLUS A GROUND)

1 With the power still off, connect the black and white wires to the end of the GFCI labeled LINE. Loop each wire around the terminal screws—black to the gold screw, white to the silver screw, and green to the ground screw in the outlet. Wrap the wire around the screw in a clockwise direction and tighten the screw.

2 Wrap electrical tape around the outside of the outlet (covering screw terminals).

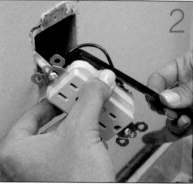

3 Gently fold the wires back into the outlet box in a zigzag pattern.

4 Screw through the ears to reconnect to the box.

5 Turn on the power. Use a non-contact voltage tester to test that the power is working.

6 Press the Test button—it should pop out the Reset button and trip the outlet. Test that the power is tripped with a circuit test. If it has, press the Reset button, which will pop out the Test button, untrip the GFCI, and restore electricity to the circuit.

7 Screw the cover plate back on the outlet.

IF YOUR OUTLET HAS FOUR WIRES (PLUS TWO GROUNDS)

1 Shut the power off from the service panel.

2 Test that the power is off at the outlet with a non-contact voltage tester.

3 Connect the *incoming* black/white wires (that you've identified with masking tape) to the end of the GFCI labeled LINE. Loop each wire around the terminal screw—black to the gold screw, white to the silver screw, and green to the ground screw in the outlet. Wrap the wire around the screw in a clockwise direction and tighten it.

4 Connect the remaining *outgoing* black/white wires to the end of the GFCI labeled LOAD.

5 For the grounds, take a short length of ground wire and make a jumper. Connect one end of the jumper to the ground screw. Bunch the grounds together, including the other end of the jumper, twist the wires with pliers, and cap them with a wire nut.

6 Wrap electrical tape around the outside of the outlet (covering screw terminals).

7 Gently fold the wires back into the outlet box in a zigzag pattern.

8 Screw through the ears to reconnect to the box.

9 Screw the cover plate back on the outlet.

10 Turn on the power. Use a non-contact voltage tester to make sure that the power is working.

11 Press the Test button—it should pop out the Reset button and trip the outlet. Test that the power is tripped with a circuit test. If it is, press the Reset button, which will pop out the Test button and untrip the GFCI, restoring electricity to the circuit.

Install a Wall-Mounted Towel Warmer

WHAT YOU'LL NEED

Soft-wire towel warmer with mounting hardware

Nail-set (or nail punch) **and hammer**

Drill driver

Small wood bit for pilot hole*

Newspaper or large towel

Pencil

Level

Electronic stud finder

* If applicable

Imagine a warm, cozy towel ready for you as you come out of the shower—what a luxury. But wait, there's more: drying delicates, wet jackets, gloves, and bathing suits—not to mention preventing mildew and odors from accumulating on damp clothing.

Easy-to-install plug-in towel warmers are available in many sizes and styles. They do use electricity, but a lot less than a dryer will. Or, for minimal energy consumption, you can put it on a timer that heats your towels just before your morning shower.

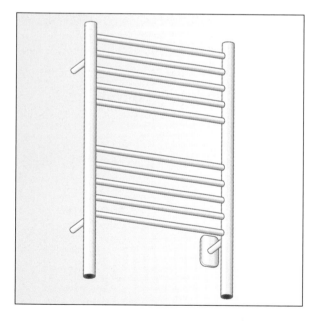

CONSIDER THIS

- Soft-wired (plug-in) towel warmers must be on a GFCI outlet. If you do not have a GFCI outlet see "Install a GFCI" on page 116.

- Choose a location for the warmer where an outlet is in close proximity.

- Hard-wired towel warmers should be installed by a professional.

- Towel warmer installations will vary—it's best to follow manufacturer's instructions and safety precautions.

PREP WORK

- Protect the floor underneath where you'll be installing the towel warmer with a large towel or newspaper.
- Plug in the warmer to make sure it's functioning properly before mounting it.
- With a stud finder, check to see if the area where you want to mount the warmer is over a stud. Mounting into a stud is preferred, but not necessary.

THE PROJECT

1 Attach the mounting brackets onto the warmer ends first, and then raise the towel warmer to the wall and decide on an appropriate height. Use a level to make sure it's level.

2 With a pencil, mark the screw holes through the mounting bracket onto the wall. Move any bracket covers out of the way to do this. Set the warmer aside.

3 Poke a nail-set into the screw marks to make small holes, and then tap in your anchors. If you hit a stud, drill a small pilot hole into the stud.

4 Screw the mounting brackets into your anchors or stud.

5 With the mounting brackets securely in place, raise the towel warmer to the wall and align it with the mounts. Use the provided locking hardware to secure the warmer to the mounts, and tighten them all down.

6 Slide any bracket covers over the mounts.

7 Plug in the unit.

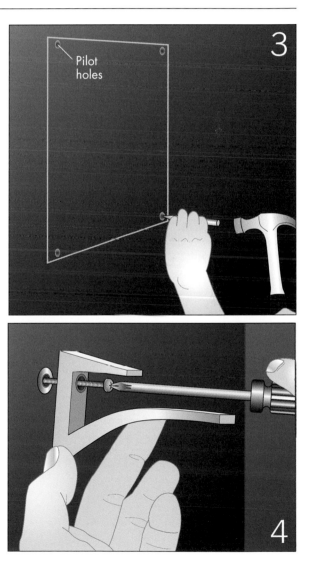

Pilot holes

Part 3

Intensive Treatment

Sinks

When fixing your faucet, sink, or vanity just won't do, *out with the old and in with the new* are the types of projects you'll find in this chapter.

Install a New Faucet and Pop-up

WHAT YOU'LL NEED

New faucet including pop up and drain, tailpiece, P-trap, and adapter (if applicable—preferably PVC or ABS with slip-joint fittings)

Tongue-and-groove pliers

Adjustable wrench

Basin wrench

Close quarter hacksaw or reciprocating saw with 6-inch bimetal blade*

Flashlight

Pillow or large kneeling pad

Small bucket

Old knife

Penetrating oil

Scour pad and rags

New stainless-steel braided water supply lines*

Teflon tape and/or pipe joint compound

Plumber's putty*

Silicone caulking

Caulking gun

* If applicable

Sometimes, the hardest part of installing a new faucet is removing the old one. Mineral deposits build up around old fittings, making it tough to disconnect the faucet from the sink deck. Be prepared to go to battle with your old faucet if it's been there a while, especially if you have hard water.

CONSIDER THIS

The most important detail to know when choosing a new faucet is what kind of faucet your sink/vanity can accommodate. Are you mounting into your sink or your vanity? How many holes does it have? What is the spread between the holes (the hole pattern or hole spread)? The most common hole pattern for a bathroom faucet is 4 inches, but it could be a single hole, or an 8-inch spread or greater (known as *widespread*). It helps to take a photo of your old faucet to help with choosing a new one, or take the old faucet with you to the store.

Spout length and height are crucial elements, because they affect how the water falls in the sink. The depth of your basin will also affect how the water falls. Keep in mind that the higher the spout and the shallower the basin, the more the water will splash outside the sink.

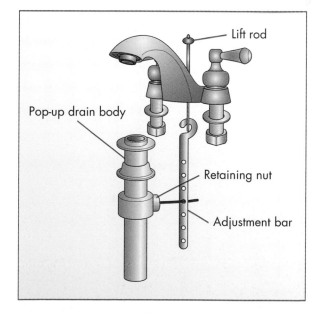

Lift rod

Pop-up drain body

Retaining nut

Adjustment bar

Typically, bathroom faucets are sold with a new pop-up and drain body. However, if your pop-up and drain are in good condition and have the same finish as the new faucet, you can leave them as is.

If you'll be changing your pop-up, it's best to purchase a new tailpiece and P-trap as well. Make sure you buy the right size—bring the old one with you to be sure of pipe diameter, length, and overall setup and length.

This installation uses PVC or ABS drain pipes and P-traps with compression-type slip-joint fittings. For more information, see the sidebar "Working with Drains and Traps" on pages 130 and 131.

Working under a sink can disorient your sense of *lefty loosey, righty tighty.* Make sure you're unscrewing the old parts in the right direction.

With any faucet, always read the manufacturer's installation instructions and safety precautions.

PREP WORK

TO REMOVE THE OLD FAUCET

- Clear away everything from under your sink for a clutter-free work space.

- Set a flashlight under the faucet and place a pillow or kneeling pad under you to work comfortably.

- Shut off the water from the shut-off valves.

- Turn the water on at the faucet to relieve pressure.

- Unscrew the water supply line from the faucet and shut-off valves (a).

- Spray the mounting nuts with penetrating oil and let it soak in (b).

- With a basin wrench, unscrew the mounting nuts (c).

- Loosen the clevis screw on the pop-up.

- Pull out the old faucet.

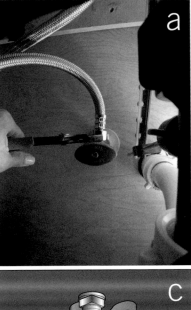

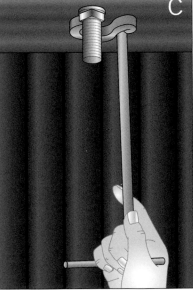

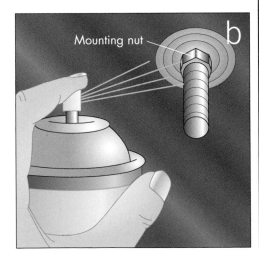

TO REPLACE THE OLD POP-UP AND DRAIN

- Unscrew the retaining nut and pull out the pivot ball/rod to the pop-up

- Unscrew and remove the P-trap (d). (Be aware that mucky water will be in the trap—have a bucket handy to dump it.) Plug up the stub-out pipe coming from the wall with a rag. (See the sidebar "Working with Drains and Traps" on pages 130 and 131.)

- Spray the sink locknut holding the rubber gasket to the sink with penetrating oil. Also spray the drain flange.

- Unscrew the locknut.

- Unscrew the drain flange. Often this part won't budge—you may need to cut the drain pipe just above the T-connector and locknut. You can do this with a close quarter hacksaw or reciprocating saw with a metal blade (e).

- Pull out the old pop-up.

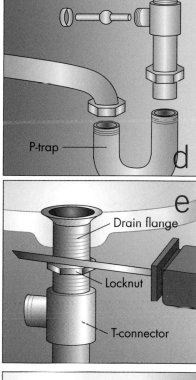

P-trap

d

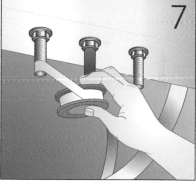

e

Drain flange

Locknut

T-connector

THE PROJECT

INSTALL THE NEW FAUCET

1 Read your faucet's instructions and safety precautions. Acquaint yourself with the faucet parts.

2 Clean away residue on your sink or vanity that may remain from the old faucet with a scour pad.

3 Assemble your faucet as directed in its instructions.

4 A faucet will use either a gasket or plumber's putty to create a seal between it and the deck (the top side of the sink or counter). Insert the gasket as directed, or apply plumber's putty under the faucet. (Roll room-temperature putty in your hands to make a ½ inch rope. Press it around the perimeter of the faucet—enough so that when you press the faucet in place, excess squeezes out.)

5 Guide the faucet into the deck holes. Orient it so the handles and spout are facing the right direction. If using putty, press firmly.

6 Thread and tighten the faucet nuts under the sink with a basin wrench. Remove any excess putty that may squeeze out.

7 Looking from underneath the sink, wrap Teflon tape clockwise around the inlet threads. (It's the same direction as you'll be tightening the supply lines.)

8 Screw the supply lines to the inlets with a basin wrench. Then screw them to the shut-off valves with an adjustable wrench or pliers. Don't let the lines spin as you're tightening them.

INSTALL THE NEW DRAIN, POP-UP, AND P-TRAP

There are numerous trap and drain setups. The following steps cover a typical pop-up, trap, and drain configuration. For more in-depth information about various trap and drain scenarios see "Working with Drains and Traps" on pages 130 and 131.

9 Put a bead of plumber's putty or silicone adhesive around the underside of the drain flange and press it into the drain hole. Wipe away any excess that squeezes out.

10 Slip the locknut, washer, and rubber gasket onto the top of the drain body (in that order, so when screwed in place, the rubber gasket will press against the sink surface).

11 Apply Teflon tape or pipe joint compound to the threads of the drain body. Under the sink, insert the threaded end of the drain body into the drain flange and screw it in tight. Then tighten the locknut with tongue-and-groove pliers until it's snug against the sink. Do not over-tighten. Be sure that when it's tight, the hole for the pop-up (T-connector hole) faces the back of the sink.

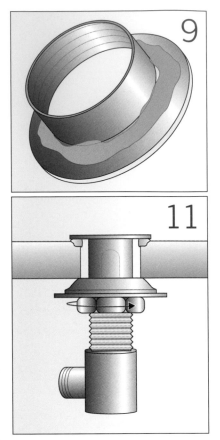

Plumber's Putty

Plumber's putty is a claylike substance that's used to create water-tight seals and a cushioned bedding between plumbing fixtures and other surfaces (for example, a faucet to a sink, or toilet to the floor). It also lightly adheres these surfaces to one another.

This putty is worked by hand to conform to the shape of whatever it is you're working on. I like to take a glob of it and roll it between my hands to create a ½-inch-long rope. Then I press off pieces of it along the perimeter of the plumbing part until there's a bead of it all the way around the outer surface.

When you press the part in place and tighten it down, excess putty will squeeze out. Simply wipe it away with your fingertips.

When working with this product make sure it's at room temperature. If it's too cold, it won't be malleable enough to shape—but it sure will give you an intense arm workout!

12 Drop the pop-up into the drain hole with the small hole on the end of the stopper facing the T-connector hole.

13 Insert the pivoting rod into the hole of the tailpiece (T-connector). Catch the hole of the stopper with the rod.

14 Screw on the retaining nut—tighten it, but still allow pivot rod movement.

15 Insert the lift rod from the top of the faucet, and then from below, attach the clevis strap (with the clevis screw) to the lift rod.

16 Have the spring-clip in hand. With the lift rod down (and pop-up up), guide the pivot rod through the spring-clip and then through the hole in the clevis strap that the pivot rod lines up with.

17 Check that the pop-up is aligned properly; pulling up on the lift rod should make the stopper go down and vice versa. Fine-tune if necessary by loosening the clevis screw and adjusting the lift rod position.

18 Test-fit the tailpiece with the P-trap and stub-out. You may need to shorten, lengthen, or add an angled adapter for the P-trap to meet the stub-out. It may take a little back-and-forth to figure out proper alignment.

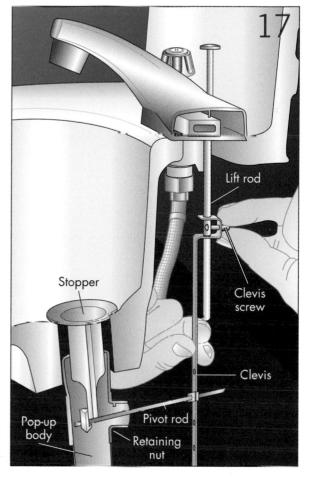

17

Lift rod

Stopper

Clevis screw

Pop-up body

Pivot rod

Retaining nut

Clevis

19 When the tailpiece, P-trap, and stub-out setup is configured, screw the tailpiece to the T-connector (first apply Teflon tape or pipe joint compound to the threads), then slide down the slip joint washers and nuts and hand-tighten them until snug.

20 Turn on the water from the shut-off valves and check for leaks.

21 Remove the aerator and turn on the faucet.

22 Fill the sink with water, testing the hot and cold. Check for leaks.

23 Push down the pop-up, empty the sink, and check for leaks again.

24 Replace the aerator. You're done!

Working with Drains and Traps

Take a moment to check out your sink drain pipes. Basically, you'll see a pipe that has a deep curve in it, which is the P-trap ("P" because of its shape). The trap's purpose is to create a barrier between your home and sewer gasses. It "traps" them through a water reservoir in that curve. Coincidentally, it will also "trap" your earring that falls down the drain, but that's not its intended purpose (although we're grateful!).

Old homes generally have galvanized drain pipes with brass fittings while newer homes use PVC or ABS.

Changing out all the old drains and traps is recommended if you're replacing your sink or faucet, especially if they're galvanized pipe. Take extra care with old and rusted pipes—they can break off unexpectedly while you're working on them. You'll want to cut out the old metal P-trap from the stub-out, because unscrewing it will be next to impossible. It's easiest to cut on the threads of the stub-out (the thinnest point). Use a reciprocating saw with a metal blade. This is not an easy cut if you're working under a vanity and quarters are tight and awkward. Another option is to use a close quarter hacksaw—and a lot of elbow grease.

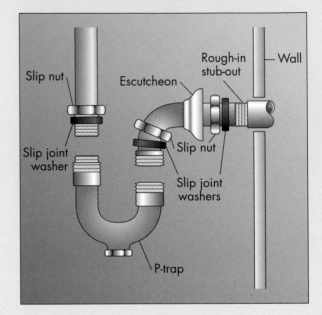

After the old P-trap is removed, you'll need to clean the stub-out. Use an old knife to scrape away the built-up residue inside the pipe. (It ain't pretty.) This will help prevent future clogs. You can now use a Fernco coupling (a short rubber section of pipe) that will adapt the old galvanized stub-out to a trap.

Unless aesthetics need be considered, PVC or ABS pipes are easiest to work with. If pipes are exposed, like under a pedestal sink, chrome-coated and other special-finish pipes are preferred.

Slip-joint-type compression fittings on P-traps create a seal with a plastic washer (or ferrule) and nut. Simply slide the washer toward the pipe end and tighten the nut over the threads. No Teflon or pipe joint compound is necessary. However, any threaded pipes that don't have this washer will need tape or glue around the threads when joined.

Often you'll need to cut or extend pipes so they align properly under the sink. Know that a pipe should extend at least an inch past the washer to prevent leaks. Never force drain and P-trap parts together. They'll likely end up leaking. If an off-center stub-out or an unruly drain setup is making you crazy, there are many options out there to make it right: flexible rubber or plastic traps, 45-degree and 90-degree angled elbows, adapters, and tailpiece extensions.

Bathroom pipes are typically 1½ inches in diameter, but this can vary. It's always best to bring old parts with you when shopping for proper size and overall drain setup.

Fernco coupling

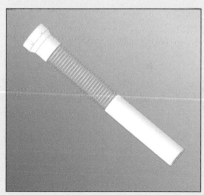

Flexible plastic P-trap

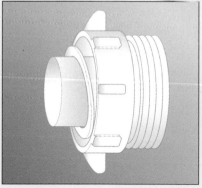

PVC reducer

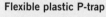

Flexible tailpiece extension

Install a New Drop-in Sink

WHAT YOU'LL NEED

New drop-in sink

Basin wrench

Screwdrivers

Drill/driver

Tongue-and-groove pliers

Adjustable wrench

Folding handsaw fitted with a 6-inch reciprocating metal blade

Close quarter hacksaw or reciprocating saw with 6-inch bimetal blade*

Jigsaw (with blade according to your countertop material)

⅜-inch drill bit for jigsaw starter hole

Utility knife

Scraper or putty knife

Safety glasses

Flashlight

Pillow or large kneeling pad

Small bucket

Scour pad and rags

Penetrating oil

Cardboard

Level

Penetrating oil

Pencil

Tape measure

Drain adapter*

Faucet including pop-up and drain, tailpiece, P-trap, and adapter

PVC or ABS with slip-joint fittings*

New stainless-steel braided water supply lines*

Teflon tape

Plumber's putty*

Pipe joint compound

Silicone adhesive

Silicone caulking

* If applicable

Whether your existing sink is chipped and worn or you just want to update the look of your bathroom, the choices of drop-in sinks today are plentiful and dazzling. Hammered copper, brushed nickel, natural stone, and glass, as well as your traditional porcelain and cast iron, are just some of the materials you can choose from. Because drop-in sinks are "self-rimming," installation is quite straightforward.

CONSIDER THIS

When choosing a new drop-in sink, you have to know the following:

• Do you need a sink with faucet holes, or does your faucet mount to your vanity? If so, what's the hole pattern?

• What is the size of the cutout for your existing sink? You must choose a sink that size or larger (unless you're replacing the vanity as well).

• Is it truly a "drop-in," meaning it's self-rimming? This naturally makes it a simple and compatible replacement to your existing vanity.

If your vanity countertop is natural stone or tiled, I recommend finding a sink with the same dimensions as the old.

If adding a new faucet, just pull out the old sink with the faucet still attached. If you have plans for the old faucet, like recycling it, it's easier to remove the faucet from the sink once it's pulled out.

If you need to modify the sink cutout of your vanity, count on a more time-consuming project.

Make sure you buy the right size tailpiece and P-trap—bring the old one with you for size and overall setup and length.

With any sink, always read manufacturer's installation instructions and safety precautions.

PREP WORK

- Before removing the old sink, clear away the space under the vanity.

- Under the vanity, check to see if there are any mounting clips holding the sink in place. If so, spray them with penetrating oil, and then unscrew them.

- From above the sink, you'll need to use a knife to cut through any silicone adhesive or caulking that's gluing the sink to the vanity. Protect the countertop with cardboard. With a utility knife, cut around the perimeter of the sink. You'll likely need a more aggressive cutting tool; if so, use a handsaw with a reciprocating blade (a).

- Shut off the water from the valves and turn on the faucet to relieve any pressure.

- Unscrew the water lines from the shut-off valves (if the faucet is mounted to the sink).

- Unscrew the top nut on the P-trap to disconnect the tailpiece (b). If this nut won't budge, you may need to cut it out. With a reciprocating saw or close quarter hacksaw, cut the old tailpiece above the P-trap. Remove the rest of the old P-trap and its tailpiece. (Be aware that mucky water will be in the P-trap—have a bucket handy to dump it.) With the P-trap removed, plug the stub-out with a rag. See the sidebar "Working with Drains and Traps" on pages 130 and 131.

- You should now be able to pull out the old sink (c).

- Wipe away any old debris on the countertop with a scour pad. You may need to use a scraper to remove the silicone.

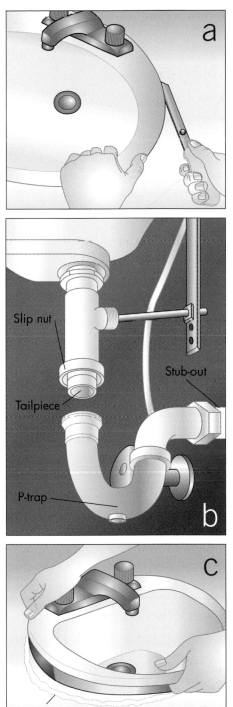

Slip nut

Stub-out

Tailpiece

P-trap

Silicone adhesive

THE PROJECT

PREPARE THE CUTOUT IN THE VANITY

1 If your new sink is the same dimensions as your old sink, verify that it fits the same cutout. If it does fit, you can skip to Step 5.

2 If your new sink has a different shape or is larger than the old cutout, you'll need to modify the existing hole. The sink should come with a cutout template. Center this template over the vanity as directed, and trace the shape. Typically, a sink is centered to the vanity from side to side and back to front. If there is no template, turn the sink upside down and center it over the hole, and then trace the sink. Remove the sink, and then trace another hole ½ inch inside the one you just made—this will be your cut line.

3 Use a drill bit to make a small starter hole for your jigsaw blade. Make the hole about an inch inside your cut line. Insert the jigsaw and start to cut the cut line.

4 Test-fit the sink. Make any adjustments.

PREPARE THE SINK, FAUCET, DRAIN, AND P-TRAP

5 If your faucet mounts to the sink, follow the manufacturer's instructions and install it now. Work with the sink on a padded surface. If your faucet mounts to the vanity deck, install it now. See "Install a New Faucet and Pop-up" on page 125.

6 Put a bead of plumber's putty or silicone adhesive around the underside of the drain flange and press it into the drain hole. Be sure to wipe away any excess that squeezes out.

7 Slip the locknut, washer, and rubber gasket onto the top of the drain body (in that order, so when screwed in place, the rubber gasket will press against the sink surface).

8 Apply Teflon tape or pipe joint compound to the threads of the drain body, and then from the underside of the sink, insert the threaded end of the drain body into the drain flange and screw it in tight. Then tighten the locknut, washer, and rubber gasket with tongue-and-groove pliers until it's snug up against the sink. Do not over-tighten. Be sure that when it's tight, the hole for the pop-up (T-connector hole) faces the back of the sink.

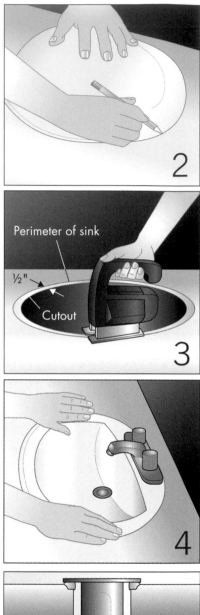

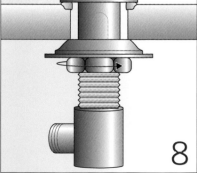

9 Attach the pop-up linkage (the part that hooks up the stopper to the pop-up). See "Install a New Faucet and Pop-up" on page 125.

10 With the sink still face side down, apply a bead of silicone adhesive around the underside of the sink's rim.

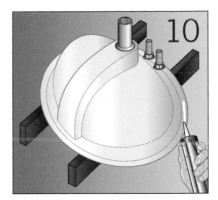

DROP IN THE SINK AND HOOK UP THE FAUCET AND DRAIN

11 Carefully place the sink into the cutout, being sure it's centered. Press it down firmly and wipe away any excess. Let it set.

12 Connect the water supply line from the faucet to the shut-off valves.

13 Test-fit the tailpiece, P-trap, and stub-out. You may need to shorten, lengthen, or add an angled adapter for the P-trap to meet the stub-out. It may take a little back-and-forth movement to figure out proper alignment.

14 When the tailpiece, P-trap, and stub-out setup is configured, screw the tailpiece to the T-connector (first apply Teflon tape or pipe joint compound to the threads), then slide down the slip joint washers and nuts and hand-tighten them until snug.

15 Turn on the water from the shut-off valves and check for leaks.

16 Remove the aerator and turn on the faucet, testing the hot and cold.

17 Fill the sink with water. Check for leaks.

18 Push down the pop-up, emptying the sink and checking for leaks again.

19 Replace the aerator, turn on the faucet, and check for leaks. Nice job!

Install a Pedestal Sink

WHAT YOU'LL NEED

New pedestal sink

Drill/driver

Drill bit to pilot hole lag screws

Masonry bit, bolts, and anchors (for tiled walls and/or floor bolted pedestals—see the sink's installation instructions)

Basin wrench

Screwdrivers

Rachet wrench and socket for bolts*

Tongue-and-groove pliers

Adjustable wrench

Circular saw or handsaw

Drywall patching materials (newspaper or old towel, utility knife, nylon mesh tape, spackle, 4-inch putty knife, and fine sandpaper)

2 two-by-fours cut to pedestal stand height*

1 two-by-six, two-by-eight, or two-by-ten (see the sink's installation instructions for blocking)

2 fender washers and 2, 2½-inch lag screws

Safety glasses

Flashlight*

Pillow or large kneeling pad

Large bucket*

Rags

Penetrating oil*

Level

Pencil

Marker

Tape measure

Faucet including pop-up and drain, tailpiece, P-trap, and adapter*—chrome coated or special finish with slip-joint fittings

Continued on next page

I love pedestal sinks. They offer an elegant look to any bathroom—from vintage to modern. Pedestal sinks are especially suited for half baths where a vanity might take over the space. As far as functionality, well, that's another story. If you keep a lot of stuff in your bathroom, you've just lost all that hidden cabinet space. And what about on top of the vanity? A tissue box, French milled guest soaps, an Elmo toothbrush holder—where you gonna put 'em all now?

That said, if a pedestal sink works for your bathroom space and lifestyle, here's something else to keep in mind: Be prepared for one tedious install. Spot on measurements, exposed plumbing, heavy yet fragile parts, and so on all make a pedestal installation one where fudging isn't an option.

CONSIDER THIS

Before getting started, look under your sink at where your stub-out and shut-off valves are set up. A pedestal sink needs the stub-out and shut-offs to be in a triangular configuration. If yours is not set up this way, hire a licensed plumber to rough in a new drain and supply lines that will accommodate a pedestal sink.

I recommend working with a partner on this project so that you have help lifting and steadying the pedestal parts.

When purchasing a new pedestal, buy one with a hole set up to match your faucet choice.

You'll want to purchase chrome or special-finish valves, trap, and drain pipes to match your faucet because they'll be exposed.

Pedestal sinks come in two parts: the stand (or pedestal) and the basin (or bowl). Vintage pedestals were made of enameled cast iron, but today they're typically made of vitreous china (a type of porcelain). There are some mixed-matter pedestals where a china basin rests in a wrought-iron stand—pretty, but pricey.

WHAT YOU'LL NEED

Continued from previous page

2 quarter-turn angle stop shut-off valves

Escutcheons for waste line and shut-off valves

New stainless-steel braided water supply lines

Teflon tape

Plumber's putty*

Silicone caulking

Drywall saw

* If applicable

Many companies offer installation instructions online. I recommend getting your hands on your pedestal's instructions in advance of your project to help plan ahead (if, say, it has to be ordered).

Be careful handling the pedestal and basin. Work on a padded surface and do not over-tighten bolts. The last thing you want to hear is that dreaded *clink* of the porcelain cracking.

Pedestal sink installations vary. It's always best to follow the manufacturer's instructions and safety precautions.

PREP WORK

First you need to remove the existing vanity and sink. (See "Install a New Vanity and Vessel Sink" on page 141.)

Unlike pedestals from years past, the stand doesn't actually support all the basin weight. Typically, the basin is mounted to a wall and requires proper blocking to bear its weight—a two-by mounted between studs will provide this support. If your plumber roughs in new plumbing for your pedestal, it's a good time to install blocking while the wall is open. If no rough-in work is necessary, you'll have to cut open the wall to build this support.

Typically, cement board and tile walls do not require additional blocking, as long as you use proper masonry anchors and screws.

- To install blocking behind drywall, check the manufacturer's pedestal height (average 29 to 35 inches) as well as the height and width of the basin itself. Use these measurements to determine the size of your blocking (likely a two-by-six or greater) and how many studs they need to be installed between.

- Mark for the opening on the wall where you'll cut out the drywall. The left and right side cuts will be determined by how spread apart the bolt holes are. Locate the studs that will accommodate this, being mindful that stub-out is at the center.

- For the top cut, measure up from the floor and mark your sink's height using a level. Determine your bottom cut by adding 3 inches to your two-by (so for two-by-six blocking, measure down 9 inches). Trace your opening on the wall with a pencil and cut out the section of drywall with a drywall saw—it's easiest to use the stud as a guide when cutting your vertical lines.

- Cut two 3-inch two-by-four blocks and screw them to the bottom ends of each stud in the opening. These will act as supports for the blocking.

- Cut your two-by blocking the distance between the studs. Wedge the two-by between the studs, on the flat side, and resting on the two-by-four blocks. *Toenail* screw the blocking to the studs (a). **Note:** Toenailing wood means joining wood together with screws or nails by driving them at approximately a 45° angle. This method is often used to join two-by to one another at a right angle.

- Patch the opening. (See "Patch Holes in Drywall" on page 52.)

THE PROJECT

PREPARE THE P-TRAP AND INSTALL SHUT-OFF VALVES AND FAUCET

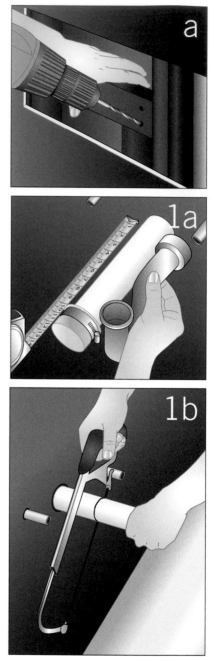

1 Get the measurement of the distance between the wall and the sink drain. This will be in your installation instructions. This measurement will tell you how far out the stub-out and trap need to come in order to meet the drain body (a). Using this measurement as a reference, hold the P-trap, waste arm, and elbow (temporarily fitted together) up against the stub-out and determine where you'll need to cut it. Mark it and use a hacksaw to cut the PVC pipe (b). Be sure to make a straight cut, but don't apply forceful downward pressure when cutting.

2 Assuming you've had two ½-inch copper supply lines roughed in, install the shut-off valves. With the water shut off at the water main, remove the stops your plumber capped the lines with—have a large bucket handy to catch the water that comes out.

3 Install the shut-off valves. (See "Replace a Shut-off Valve" on page 168.)

4 Apply plumber's putty or silicone adhesive around the bottom of the drain flange and install the drain to the basin. (See "Install a New Drop-in Sink" on page 132.)

5 Install the faucet and the pop-up linkage to the basin. (See "Install a New Faucet and Pop-up" on page 125.)

INSTALL THE PEDESTAL

6 If your basin has a mounting plate that fastens to the wall, mount it now according to the height and placement indicated in the manufacturer's instructions. Set the basin onto the mounting plate and screw it in place. Do not over-tighten. Skip any basin mounting procedures in the following steps.

7 If your sink does not have a mounting plate, set the stand in place and carefully place the basin on it. **Warning:** It will not be stable. If the sink is very large, prop two two-by-fours under the basin for temporary supports. It's best work to with a partner who can steady it while you continue installing. Make sure the basin is level, square, and centered on the stand.

8 Mark the wall with the basin bolt holes through the back of the sink. Mark the base footprint on the floor as well as any bolt holes if necessary.

9 Remove the stand and basin, and drill the bolt holes into the wall.

10 Put the stand and basin back in place and bolt the basin to the wall. Do not over-tighten.

11 Prop the two-by-fours under the basin (if needed) and remove the stand.

12 Slide the escutcheon over the waste line. Install the P-trap and drain setup. Connect the water lines.

13 With the P-trap and drain setup, test-fit the stand to make sure they tuck behind the stand.

14 Tighten the drain fittings. Remove the stand to make it easier.

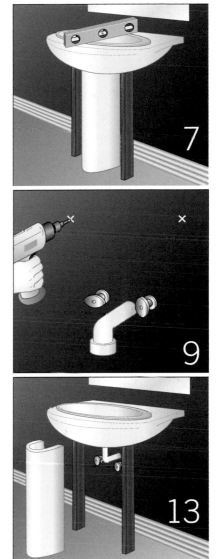

15 Drill the bolt holes in the floor for the stand (if necessary).

16 When the drain and P-trap are in place and tightened, turn on the water from the shut-off valves and check for leaks.

17 Remove the aerator from the faucet. Turn on the faucet; check hot and cold. Fill and drain the sink and check for leaks.

18 Apply a bead of caulking to the top of the stand and to the floor where the stand sits.

19 Slip the stand under the basin—make sure it's centered and plumb. Remove the two-by-fours.

20 Bolt the stand to the floor (if applicable).

21 Put a bead of silicone caulking between the basin and the wall. Wow, you did it!

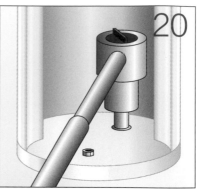

Install a New Vanity and Vessel Sink

WHAT YOU'LL NEED

New vanity and vessel sink

Screwdrivers

Drill/driver

Basin wrench

Tongue-and-groove pliers

Adjustable wrench

Hole saws (as needed for drain and pipe openings—see the sink's installation instructions)

Close quarter hacksaw or reciprocating saw with 6-inch bimetal blade*

Pry bar

Safety glasses

Flashlight

Pillow or large kneeling pad

Drywall patching materials (newspaper or old towel, utility knife, nylon mesh tape, spackle, 4-inch putty knife, and fine sandpaper)

Small bucket

Rags

Penetrating oil

Level

Pencil

Tape measure

Faucet including pop-up and drain, tailpiece, P-trap, and adapter

PVC or ABS with slip-joint fittings*

Wood shims*

New stainless-steel braided water supply lines*

Hinged escutcheons for waste line and shut-offs*

Continued on next page

The look of vanities has really changed over the past decade. Today they can seem more like a piece of fine furniture than a cabinet holding a sink. Their size and profiles range from dainty to massive, making them an option for just about any bathroom.

Another stylish addition to the vanity is the vessel sink. The first time I saw one it took my breath away. First it reminded me of the old-fashioned pitcher and wash basins you'd see set on a Victorian dressing table. Yet the innovative materials some use, like crackled glass or travertine, blend old world and modern to perfection.

Then I thought, "How the heck is this thing plumbed? It's a bowl sitting on a piece of furniture with water running through it, for God's sake!" Actually, they're often more simple to install than a traditional drop-in sink and vanity.

CONSIDER THIS

Tearing out your old sink and vanity will require wall and possibly molding repairs, especially if your new vanity is smaller and/or footed.

A new vanity may be an opportunity to increase your storage space and counter surface. You may also choose one that's higher, for comfort. If it's going bigger, be mindful of things like light switches and outlets that may interfere with a larger vanity. You also want to avoid crowding the toilet or obstructing the swing of the door.

Know how high your waste line is on the wall and account for the dip in the P-trap to make sure it can fit properly in the vanity.

WHAT YOU'LL NEED

Continued from previous page

Teflon tape

Plumber's putty*

Pipe joint compound

Silicone adhesive

Silicone caulking

* If applicable

A vessel sink may be mounted directly above the countertop, requiring only a hole cut in the counter for the drain, or partially recessed, which would require a larger cutout. Sometimes manufacturers recommend a mounting ring that sits on the counter and raises the sink for a partial drop-in effect.

Vessel sinks may or may not have an overflow. If yours does, it should have a pop-up faucet and drain assembly. However, most vessel sinks do not have an overflow that calls for a vessel-style faucet and grid drain (*grid* describes the pattern over the drain hole that stops debris from going down the drain).

The following installation addresses an above-the-counter installation with a no-overflow sink, a vessel-style grid drain, and deck-mounted faucet with no pop-up.

PREP WORK

It's easiest to remove the sink and countertop all in one piece. You may disconnect them later for recycling or repurposing.

TO REMOVE THE OLD SINK AND VANITY

- Clear out all your under-the-sink stuff.
- Turn off the water at the shut-off valves.
- Set a flashlight in the cabinet for better visibility. Disconnect the water lines from the shut-off valves and the P-trap from the waste line. Remove any escutcheons. Plug the waste line stub-out with a rag or cap (a).

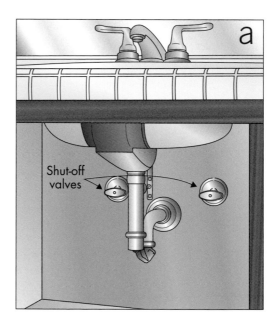

- Under the cabinet, look for screws holding the countertop to the cabinet base. Unscrew them all. If there are no screws, it may be simply held down with silicone adhesive—use a handsaw fitted with a 6-inch reciprocating metal blade to cut through the joint between the cabinet and counter. If it's nailed down, which is likely with a tile top, use a pry bar to pry up the counter (b). Cut or pry the backsplash from the wall (if applicable). If you can't seem to detach the countertop from the cabinet, it may be easier to remove them in one piece.

- Lift off the countertop from the cabinet. This will be heavy lifting, so work with a partner and be careful not to hurt your back.

- If there's floor molding, pry it off with a small pry bar.

- Look at how the cabinet is mounted into the wall—there may be screws, nails, adhesive, or all of the above. Unfasten as necessary and pull the cabinet out (c).

- Clean up the debris and begin your wall repairs. (See "Patch Holes in Drywall" on page 52.)

- After the patches are dried, it's the ideal time to prime and paint.

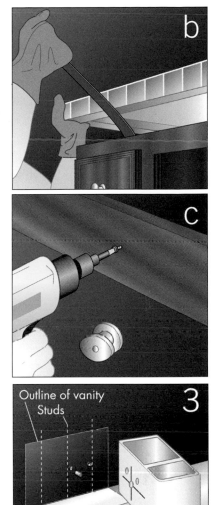

Outline of vanity
Studs

THE PROJECT

INSTALL THE VANITY CABINET

1 Trace the vanity measurements on the wall. Be mindful of where the waste line is relative to the center of the vanity.

2 Locate the wall studs and mark them with a pencil and level.

3 Measure the waste line and shut-off valves on the wall and transfer those measurements to the back of the vanity. If the back of your vanity has no back panel to it, skip to Step 6.

4 With a hole saw, cut the openings for the waste line and shut-off valves. To avoid having to remove shut-off valves, cut holes big enough to slide them through. (You'll use hinged escutcheons to finish the holes.)

5 Remove the doors from the vanity (to avoid damaging them).

6 Fit the vanity against the wall, sliding the pipes through the holes you made in the back of the vanity.

7 Make sure it's level and square. You may need to use wood shims if the wall or floor isn't level.

8 Screw the vanity into the studs through the "nailer"—the piece of wood running along the back top of the vanity. Be sure not to sink screws anywhere but into studs, as you could hit a pipe. Use 3-inch wood screws and washers.

9 If applicable, with a utility knife cut off or chisel the exposed tips of the shims (careful not to mar the floor or wall). Your cabinet may call for floor molding; if so, you may install it now using finish nails.

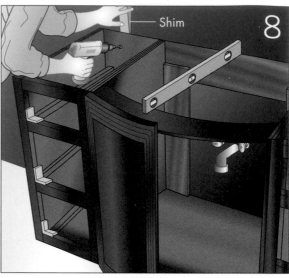

INSTALL AND PREPARE THE COUNTERTOP

10 Dry-fit the countertop onto the cabinet. When it's centered on the base, make tick marks with a pencil under the top to see exactly where you need to line up when you permanently set it in place.

11 Remove the countertop. Put a bead of silicone adhesive around the top of the base. Place the countertop onto the base, following your tick marks, line it up so it's centered, and then press it down firmly. Wipe away any excess. Let it set.

12 If the countertop holes for the sink and faucet are not yet cut out, place the vessel and faucet on the countertop and center them. Be sure they're placed far enough away from the wall to allow handle movement. Trace their location.

13 With a hole saw, cut the opening for the sink drain—this is usually 1½ inches. For the faucet, most vessel-type faucets have a single hole configuration that is either installed on the sink deck or countertop. If your sink calls for a faucet that is countertop mounted, check the manufacturer's specifications for the hole size, and drill your hole.

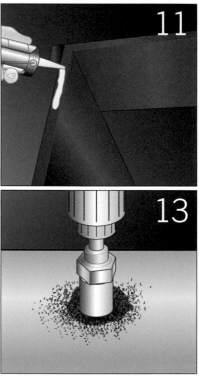

PREPARE AND INSTALL THE FAUCET AND VESSEL SINK

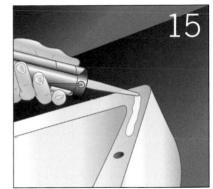

14 Install the faucet—this will involve securing a mounting nut from beneath the countertop (see "Install a New Faucet and Pop-up" on page 125). Because there is no pop-up, this installation is more simple. Hook-up the water supply lines. See your faucet's instructions for more specifications.

15 Put a bead of silicone adhesive along the flat bottom part of the sink. Set the sink onto the countertop, lining up the drain with the drain hole. Wipe away any excess. Check the sink manufacturer to see if a special adhesive is required for your sink material.

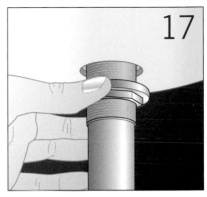

16 Place a bead of plumber's putty or silicone adhesive around the drain flange and set it into the drain hole of the sink. Press the flange firmly in the hole and wipe away the excess.

17 Under the cabinet, tighten the gasket, washer, and locknut to secure the drain body to the sink. Hook up the tailpiece, P-trap, and waste line. (See "Working With Drains and Traps" on pages 130 and 131.)

18 Turn on the water from the shut-off valves. Check for leaks at the valves and faucet connections. Remove the faucet aerator. Turn on the faucet; let it run, checking hot and cold. Check for leaks again.

19 Screw back the aerator. Screw on the doors. Admire your work!

How can I safely remove a large vanity wall mirror?

Is your old wall mirror not going to work with your cool new furniture-style vanity?

Sometimes referred to as a "builder mirror," a large, flat vanity mirror is almost always glued to the wall. Some mirrors have screws, clips, or clips and a track—if this is the case, there's probably no glue that you'll have to contend with. The question is, how do you remove a large glued mirror without cracking it, causing substantial damage to the wall or, worse yet, yourself? The answer: *Carefully!* Dealing with mirrors can be hazardous, but there are tricks to doing it safely and effectively. Practice safety first:

- Wear safety glasses, long sleeves, pants, closed shoes, and thick leather gloves.
- Make several vertical and horizontal stripes across the mirror with duct tape.
- Cover anything under the mirror with a packing blanket or heavy-duty dropcloth.
- Work with a partner.

With a utility knife, cut the seal around the mirror that may have accumulated from layers of paint. Gently wedge a putty knife behind one corner of the mirror. Now heat up the mirror with a blow dryer for several minutes (to loosen the glue). Slide piano wire behind the mirror and, working with your partner, begin sawing the wire back and forth. Reheat the mirror as you go. Little by little, you'll work through the glue. Always keep one hand against the mirror for support in case it suddenly gives way.

If this method is getting you nowhere, you may just have to break it out. The truth is, no matter how careful you are, there's always a chance that the mirror might break. Look, it's gotta go, so as long as you remove it safely, never you mind about those 7 years of bad luck. . . .

Showers

A sure way to upgrade your shower is by installing shower doors. But what if it's a leaky shower pan—rather than a leaky shower curtain—that's just not letting your shower, well, hold water? Find out how to fix both in this chapter.

Install a Shower Door

WHAT YOU'LL NEED

Two panel bypass door kit for a shower/tub enclosure

Phillips screwdriver

Nail-set (or nail punch) **and hammer**

Drill driver

Masonry bit (size as indicated by manufacturer's instructions)

Hacksaw and miter box

Protective tarp or blanket

Tape measure

Masking tape

Pencil

Metal file

Safety glasses

Level

Silicone caulking

Going from a shower curtain to a shower door is like switching from a $5.99 folding umbrella you buy from a street vendor to a 68-inch double-canopy oversized golf umbrella. The upgrade is substantial and will be obvious in both looks and performance. Finished sleek lines as well as the elimination of those awful curtain leaks are improvements that you'll appreciate every time you shower.

CONSIDER THIS

The shower will be off-limits for 24 hours or until caulking dries.

It's imperative that you're very exact in measuring the opening for the new doors.

Explore the various styles and finishes of doors before choosing one. Know that frameless and clear glass doors will make the bathroom look bigger—it'll extend the eye all the way to the shower wall as opposed to stopping at the door. These are some of the more popular designs:

- **Two-panel bypass.** Framed or frameless, these doors slide back and forth on a track.

- **Tri-panel bypass.** Same as the two-panel, but the three smaller panels can slide and stack over one another, allowing for a wider opening.

- **Bi-fold.** This door is hinged in the middle and folds onto itself when opening. For small spaces, this is great solution.

- **Swing.** These doors swing open along a full length hinge or pivot points.

The following installation addresses a two-panel bypass door kit for a shower/tub enclosure. With any shower door, always read the manufacturer's installation instructions and safety precautions.

PREP WORK

• Protect the tub with a blanket or tarp.

To determine the size door you need, properly measure the opening:

• Measure the width of the wall-to-wall opening in two places, one toward the bottom and one toward the top. The door you choose must be equal to or greater than the largest measurement.

• Measure the height of the opening, from the top of the tub rim to the top of the surround. The door you choose must be equal to or less than this measurement.

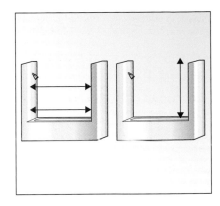

THE PROJECT

1 Verify the measurement of the wall-to-wall opening, and then subtract ⅛ inch. With a hacksaw and miter box (shown in the image on the right), cut the bottom track using this measurement. Hold the track steady when cutting to be sure to make a clean, square cut. Wear safety glasses.

2 Position the track on the center of the tub rim, with the taller side of the track facing the exterior. With a pencil, mark its position, and then temporarily secure it in place with masking tape.

3 Slip the door jambs over each end of the track. You may use a metal file to round the ends of the jambs if it helps make a tighter fit with a rounded corner. Temporarily secure them to the wall with tape.

4 With a level, plum each door jamb, and then resecure them with the tape.

5 Mark the predrilled hole locations with a marker. Remove the track and jambs.

6 Before drilling the jamb holes, use masking tape or etch the mark with a nail-set to prevent the drill bit from walking.

7 Drill the holes with a masonry bit. See the manufacturer's instructions for bit size. Never screw any holes into the tub.

8 Remove debris from the holes and gently tap in the plastic anchors with a hammer.

9 Run silicone caulk along the underside edges of the bottom track. Press the track in place, lining it up with the mark you made. Wipe away excess that oozes out. Use masking tape to prevent the track from shifting as you continue the project.

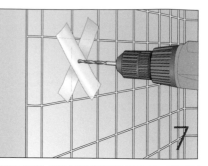

10 Slip the door jambs in place, lining up the holes. Screw the jambs to the walls, using any spacers or bumpers provided. Do not overtighten.

11 Measure the wall-to-wall opening at the top of the door jambs, and then subtract $1/16$ inch. Cut the header using this measurement. File ends if necessary for best fit.

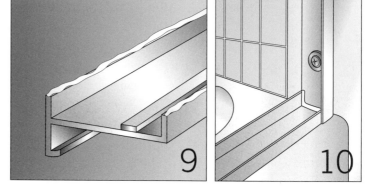

12 Install the header over the jambs—pivot it into position—it should lock in place.

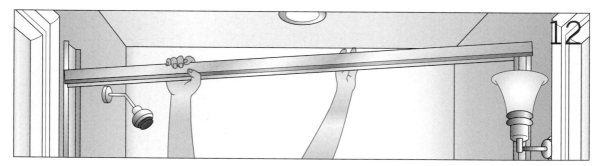

13 Install the rollers, handles, and towel bar to the doors as directed by manufacturer's instructions. Be sure to confirm the inside and outside of the glass and work on a padded surface.

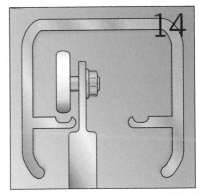

14 Standing inside the shower, lift the interior glass door into position and pivot the rollers over the groove in the header. Adjust the roller within the slot. Repeat with the exterior door.

15 Slide them against their respective door jambs. If they don't properly align against the jamb, remove the doors and adjust the position of the rollers within their slot.

16 Slide both doors to one side and secure the center panel guide in place.

17 Align any additional rubber bumpers with door panels and jamb—screw them in place.

18 Run neat beads of silicone along all places where the tracks and jambs meet the tub and walls. Smooth silicone caulk with your fingertip and wipe away any excess. Let it dry for 24 hours.

Replace a Leaky Shower Pan

WHAT YOU'LL NEED

PVC or CPE shower pan liner

Hammer

Drill/driver

Tar paper

Staples and staple gun

Cement mixing pan

Concrete hoe

Wire mesh

PVC tile shower drain (two-piece assembly)

Fernco coupler*

PVC primer and glue

Matching or coordinating shower tile for walls and floor

Worm drive or circular saw with masonry blade

Earplugs, mask, safety glasses

Utility knife

Pry bar

Cold chisel

Wood and drywall for repairs*

Galvanized roofing nails or staples

Cement board

Cement-board screws

Portland cement and sand

¾ plywood*

Large bucket

Shower drain plug

¼ inch notched trowel, mason's towel, and concrete finishing towel, floats, sponges for cement and tile work

Level

Thin-set mortar

Pea gravel

Silicone caulking

Shower pan liner adhesive

* If applicable

A shower pan isn't actually a pan at all—it's a flexible liner that creates a waterproof membrane beneath the tile and mortar of your shower stall floor. If this membrane fails, instead of it directing water down the drain, it will slowly allow water to seep out. A leaky shower pan will reveal itself through one or more of the following signs: moldy and loose tiles at the base of the shower, swollen cabinetry near the shower, water stains on the ceiling beneath the shower, and gaps where the shower walls and floor meet. Old pans were made of lead, but today a heavy-duty PVC or CPE is the optimal choice for durability as well as ease of installation.

Replacing a leaky shower pan is a great option when installing an entirely new shower stall just doesn't fit your budget. Do keep in mind that if the entire shower stall looks corroded, it's likely that the walls will be too far gone to keep, even with a new pan. In that case, tearing out the old and starting fresh is the only logical option.

CONSIDER THIS

Replacing a shower pan as demonstrated in this project entails actually building a new shower base. It will take several days to complete when you consider the labor hours and drying times of all the various steps.

Because of the nature of this project—strategically removing and replacing the bottom portion of the shower—consider it a DIY "surgical dissection." Strong skills in plumbing and masonry work, as well as *patience,* are musts for this project.

Choosing a perfect match or complementary tile is imperative for this project to achieve an attractive finished look.

Polyvinyl chloride (PVC) or chlorinated polyethylene (CPE) liner are sold by the square foot. CPE is about twice the price of PVC, but it may be worth the cost because of its ease of use. It's more malleable than PVC, which makes it easier to work with, particularly for a first-time DIYer.

While prefab solid shower floors are easier to install and less costly, your odds of finding one that will fit the exact dimensions of your older shower stall are slim.

Depending on what kind of existing shower drain you have, you may need to access it from the ceiling beneath the shower in order to fit the new drain—adding a drywall repair to the project.

This project relates to an old mortar (mud) shower stall with a plywood subfloor. This project has many steps and layers. Refer to the overview cross-section image on page 157.

PREP WORK

In order to remove the old shower pan, first you'll need to remove a few courses of wall tile because the liner extends up the wall. Once that's complete the floor tiles, mortar, and pan come out—exposing the subfloor and wall studs.

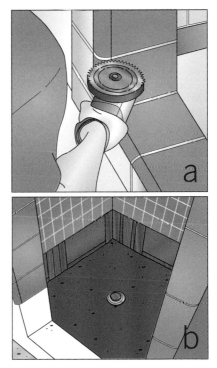

- At least 3 inches above the shower door curb (dam), or 10 inches up from the drain, locate a grout line. With a worm drive or circular saw cut at this grout line, through the tile and mortar, horizontally around the entire perimeter of the shower stall (a). Be careful *not* to damage the course of tile above this grout line. Be sure to wear a mask, ear plugs, and safety glasses. Be aware that you'll likely be cutting through wire mesh in the mud.

- With a hammer, pry bar, and cold chisel remove all the tile, mortar, and mesh until the studs are exposed.

- Continue this process along the shower floor (and curb) until the subfloor is exposed (b). Removal of the liner will vary depending on how deteriorated it is and what it's made of. It may simply break out right along with the mortar, or it may need additional efforts to remove it.

- Verify that the plywood is not rotted; if it is, it'll need to be replaced. Remove the old plywood and install new ¾-inch plywood over the floor joists. This will also involve cutting a hole in the plywood for the drain.

- Clean away any debris.

THE PROJECT

PREPARE THE NEW DRAIN

1 Unscrew or cut out the old drain with a reciprocating saw including the part that is mounted to the subfloor.

2 You'll likely need to use a Fernco flexible *coupling* (a short rubber section of pipe) to adapt the old drain pipe to the new PVC drain. To get to the drain, you may need to access it by opening up the subfloor or through the ceiling beneath the shower. With the proper pipe-to-drain adaptation, install the new drain base to the drain pipe with primer and cement (or PVC primer and cement/glue) so that it sits flat on the subfloor.

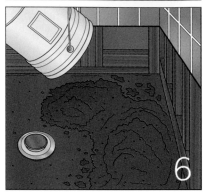

POUR THE FIRST MORTAR BED AND PREPARE THE LINER

3 Cover the drain base opening with duct tape.

4 Staple a layer of tar paper to the plywood subfloor to prevent moisture from the mortar from seeping into the wood.

5 Make the cement mortar mix (a fairly dry mix of one part Portland cement and five parts sand). In a cement mixing pan, use a concrete hoe to first mix the sand and cement together. Then slowly add water until it reaches a consistency that when you squeeze a clump in your hand, it holds its shape. If excess water squeezes out, add more sand.

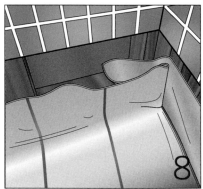

6 Fill a bucket with the mortar and begin dumping batches of it onto the tar-papered plywood. With a finish trowel, spread the mortar from the walls to the drain hole with a ¼-inch-per-foot slope toward the drain, and ending flush with the drain. Use a level and tape measure to determine this slope. It is imperative that this slope is established with this initial mortar bed; this will properly direct water toward the drain and ensure that it doesn't pool in other areas. Allow the mortar to dry for 24 hours.

7 With a utility knife cut the liner according to your shower's dimensions. Remember to account for covering the entire door curb, plus lapping up along the walls 3 inches from the top of the curb (or about 10 inches up from the drain). For larger showers, seaming may be necessary. Follow special bonding adhesive instructions.

8 Once the mortar bed has dried, test-fit the liner.

9 Remove the duct tape and apply an ample bead of silicone caulking around the drain base. Insert the locking ring bolts loosely into the drain base.

INSTALL THE LINER AND UPPER SECTION OF THE DRAIN

10 Begin placing the liner onto the mortared subfloor. When fitting the liner over the drain base, cut small Xs into the liner so the bolt heads can slide through it and the liner can snug down onto the drain. Press the liner into the silicone to ensure a seal.

11 Continue to work the liner around the entire floor, into the corners, up the walls, and over the curb. Nail or staple the liner ½ inch below the liner's edge to the studs and framing. For the corners, fold and tuck, and then nail them to the framing. **Remember:** The liner must lap up onto the walls, 3 inches above the curb. Do not nail or staple lower than ½ inch from that point—penetrating the liner anywhere lower than this point risks causing liner to leak. Also, only nail or staple on the *outside* of the curb. A special liner adhesive can be used to ensure proper fit around the curb and corners.

12 Locate the drain hole beneath the liner and cut out the opening with a utility knife (a). Be careful not to overcut. Place the locking ring (b) over the bolts and onto the drain base, and twist it counterclockwise to lock it in place. Snug down the bolts. (**Note:** It is imperative that the small weep holes remain clear from debris, silicone, or liner. These holes allow water to be properly directed down the drain.)

13 Now it's time to test the liner for leaks. Block the drain with a plug, and fill the shower base about an inch under the curb top. Let it set for several hours, and then check for leaks. The water level should not have changed.

14 Continue to install the drain. Insert the threaded drain barrel into the locking ring and screw it down to the final height of the shower floor (accounting for 1½ inches more for mortar, thinset, and tile depth).

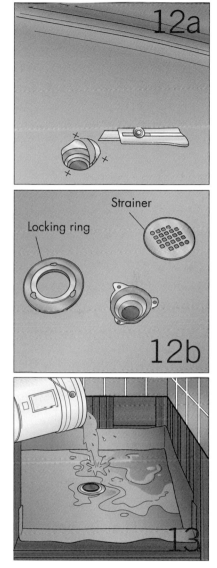

POUR THE SECOND MORTAR BED

15 First, sprinkle some pea gravel over the weep holes so they don't become clogged with the mortar. Also, plug the drain so no mortar falls down it.

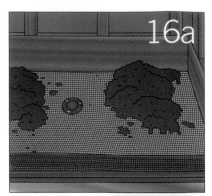

16 Now the second mortar bed can be poured in, but this time using wire mesh for reinforcement (a). This mesh should continue up along the curb and be nailed or stapled only to the *outside* of the door curb. Float the mortar toward the drain, being sure to maintain the slope. Use a straightedge to help you work the right angles of the curb (b).

TILE THE SHOWER FLOOR AND WALL

17 After the second mortar bed is completely dry, use thin-set to tile the shower floor. Spread the thin-set with a notched trowel. Begin setting the shower floor tile.

For more information about setting tile see "Tile a Tub Surround" on page 159.

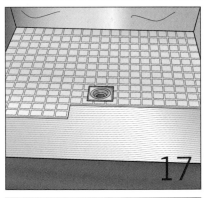

18 Once the tile is completely dry, it's time to hang the cement board to the studs. Be careful not to force the wallboard in place. Leave a ¼-inch gap between the boards and the shower floor. (You may need to hang more than one sheet of cement board to build out the wall enough from the studs to match the existing shower wall.) Be sure not to fasten the nails or screws toward the bottom of the boards where the liner laps up onto the walls. This will pierce the liner and cause leaks.

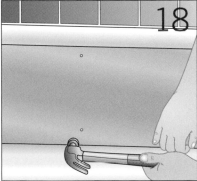

19 Apply silicone caulking all along the joints where the cement boards and shower floor meet.

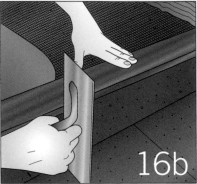

20 Tile the walls (a) and then the curb. **Note:** When tiling the curb, slightly pitch the tiles toward the inside of the shower so water will run back into the shower (b). Let them dry.

21 Grout all the tiled surfaces and then seal the tiles according to the manufacturer's recommendations. (For grouting tips, see "Replace a Damaged Tile Section" on page 93.)

22 Screw on the strainer. Wow, what an accomplishment. Congratulations on completing one of the most difficult projects in this book!

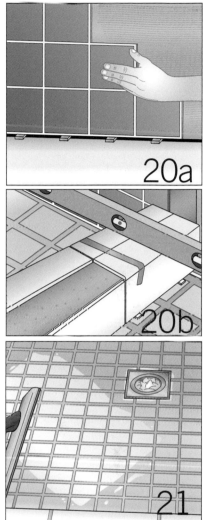

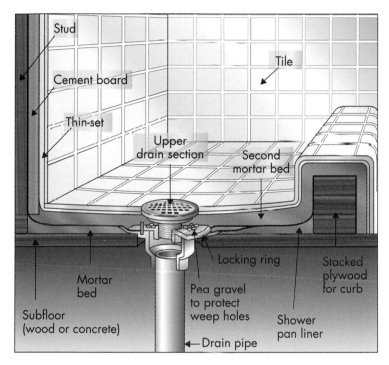

Stud

Tile

Cement board

Thin-set

Upper drain section

Second mortar bed

Locking ring

Mortar bed

Stacked plywood for curb

Subfloor (wood or concrete)

Pea gravel to protect weep holes

Shower pan liner

Drain pipe

Bathtubs

The tub itself is fine, but the tiled surround and faucet need updating.

In this chapter, you'll learn how to replace both and make your

bathtub look showroom new.

Tile a Tub Surround

WHAT YOU'LL NEED

Circular saw

Drill/driver

Masonry hole saws

Jigsaw and tile blade

Pry bar hammer

Rod saw or rotary power tool

Carbide cement board scoring knife

Utility knife

Masonry chisel

Earplugs, dust mask, safety glasses, heavy-duty gloves

Cardboard and packing blanket or protective tarp

Metal snips (for mud walls)

Cement board (or CBU)

4-foot level

Two-by-threes

Pencil and marker

Tape measure

Cement board screws

Cement board

Latex-fortified mortar

Alkali-resistant fiberglass tape

Tiles

Tile spacers

Waterproof tile mastic

Notched trowel

Nippers

Abrasion stone or file

Manual or wet blade tile cutter

Grout (unsanded for grout lines smaller than ¼ inch)

Grout sealant

Rubber float

Bucket

Synthetic tile sponge

Clean rag

Old tub tiles can really make your bathroom look outdated and dingy. But what if your tub is still in good shape? Does it all need to be torn out, tub and all? The good news is no! (And I mean *really good news*—breaking out a tub is a bear of a project.)

So if this is true for you—you have a solid-looking tub but shabby, passé tiles—a cost-efficient and aesthetically pleasing way to renew your bathroom is to retile the surround.

CONSIDER THIS

Before beginning this project, you'll need to make a diagnosis as to whether you have to: (a) take the surround down to the studs, (b) remove just the tile, or (c) tile right over the existing tile. Review the scenarios in "Prep Work" and see which approach best applies to your tub surround.

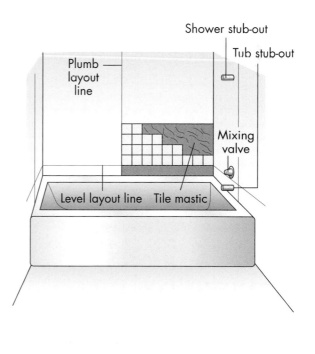

If your project requires that you replace the walls, know that installing new cement board underlayment (CBU) walls is best done with a partner. These boards are far heavier than regular drywall.

Replacing your surround is the perfect time to update your tub/shower faucet—see "Replace a Three-Handle Tub/Shower Faucet" on page 164.

This project addresses replacing a surround that needs to be removed completely—bringing it down to the studs, hanging cement board, and then tiling.

PREP WORK

- It is imperative that the tub is extremely well protected before you start this project. Use cardboard on the base of the tub and then lay out a packing blanket that covers the entire surface of the tub and tape it to the tub's ledge.

- Shut off the water from the main or from a designated shut-off valve to this bathroom.

- Remove the showerhead, temperature control knob(s), and tub spout.

- Plug the shower fitting and cap the tub stub-out—doing so will allow you to turn the water back on at the main after demolition.

- Be sure to wear protective gear—heavy-duty gloves, eye and ear protection, and a dust mask—when removing and sanding tiles and walls.

To address the existing surround, follow the method below that best fits its condition:

- **Removing the walls and tile.** Taking the walls down to the studs will be necessary if the tiles are unstable and/or the walls are not sound from either water damage or tiles that have broken away.

  - Use a circular saw to cut around the perimeter of the tiled walls, and then use a pry bar to carefully pull down the walls. Know that if your tub walls seem very thick, indicating an old mud job, removing them will be very intensive (there will be wire lath in the mortar).

  - After the studs are exposed, use a 4-foot level to check that they are plumb and on plane with one another. You may need to shim or sister studs (fastening new studs that are plumb and level to the old ones).

- **Removing just the tiles.** Sometimes, especially on old mud jobs, tiles will loosen from the walls and easily break away with a few whacks of a hammer and masonry chisel. Check the lower course of tiles on the shower body wall. Often if those tiles go easily, the rest will come a-tumblin' down.

- **Tiling over tiles.** If the walls and tiles are sound, you may tile right over them. Be aware that you will lose some cubic space. You'll need to scuff up the tile with a mechanical sander (such as an orbital or belt sander) to create a "tooth" on the smooth ceramic surface for the new tile to stick to. Be sure to wipe away all dust before tiling, and then use a strong elastic and waterproof tile adhesive.

THE PROJECT

This project assumes that the old surround has been taken down to the studs. The studs have been checked, brought to plumb, and are on plane with one another. The tub stub-out has been capped, and the showerhead pipe has been plugged. The water has been turned back on, and no leaks have occurred from demolition.

HANG THE CEMENT BOARD UNDERLAYMENT (CBU)

1 Typically, for the long wall of the tub, two sheets of CBU, cut to size, are hung horizontally and secured with cement board screws, fastening every 8 inches on the centers of the studs. **Note:** CBU should never rest directly on the tub ledge. Because of wicking action, water could soak up the CBU if the silicone joint fails and end up rotting the wood framing. Leave ¼ inch of space between the boards and the tub ledge.

2 The front and back walls will receive vertical boards, cut to size, with holes precut to accommodate the plumbing fixtures on the front wall. Holes for fixtures can be cut with masonry hole saws.

3 Prefill joints with a latex-fortified mortar, and then embed alkali-resistant fiberglass tape and smooth down and seal the joint with an additional pass of mortar. Allow the mortar to dry completely before tiling following the manufacturer's drying time.

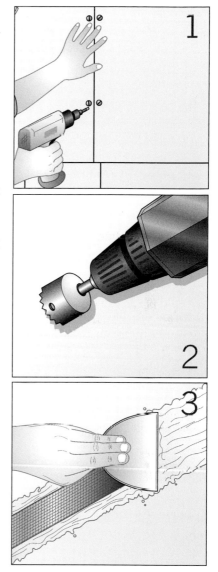

PREPARE LAYOUT FOR TILE

Because the tub will most likely not be level, you need to determine a level starting point for your first course of tile. A leveled two-by-three screwed to the wall will establish your starting point, plus give the tiles something secure to rest on as they dry. It will also act as a *story stick* (a homemade tool used to physically mark placement and layout of things like tiles and cabinets).

4 Measure up the wall from the tub ledge the height of your tile minus ½ inch. Mark a level line at this height all the way around the tub surround using a 4-foot level. Screw two-by-threes on the flat (or the 3 inch side of the two-by-three) with the top of the wood lined up with your level mark.

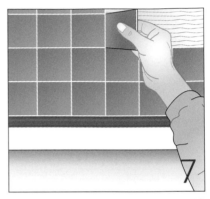

5 Establish your tile layout using this two-by-three as a story stick. Start with a full tile in one corner and dry-set a course. Now see if an unwanted sliver of tile is produced at the other end. To correct this problem, measure how much you'll need to cut from the first tile in order for the end tile to be larger. After tile spacing is established along the story stick, mark the layout along the stick with a marker.

6 Locate the closest-to-center vertical tile joint from the story stick. Use this joint to mark a plumb line up the wall.

TILE THE WALLS

7 With a notched trowel, spread the mastic in a small section at an angle. Use the story stick to line up tiles. Slightly slide each tile in place and tap it with the butt of a closed fist. Maintain uniform and straight joints using the plumb line as a guide and tile spacers as you work your way up the wall. If excess mastic squeezes through the joint, use a screwdriver to scrape it out. Keep in mind, smaller grout lines do best in wet environments. Depending on the tile, you may be able to butt the tile right next to one another, creating very thin grout lines, where no spacers are necessary. The drawback, however, is the smaller the grout line, the less room for error.

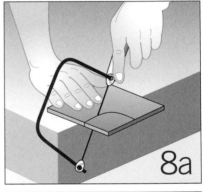

8 To cut tiles for the plumbing fixtures, use a rotary power tool or rod saw (a) to cut curves or a masonry hole saw for circles. Use nippers (b) to make small bites in the tile. Smooth-cut edges with an abrasive stone or file.

9 After the tiles have dried, remove the two-by-threes and tile the bottom course of tile. Be sure to use ¼-inch shims or spacers between these tiles and the tub ledge for a caulk joint. Be ready to make fine diagonal cuts along some of these tiles, because the tub will more than likely not be level. To do so, measure the height on each side of the space the tile will go and transfer those measurements on each side of the tile. There will be a variance in height. Draw the diagonal line across the bottom of the tile, and make the cut using a tile cutter.

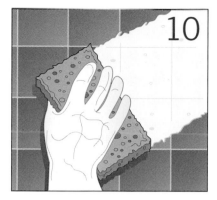

10 After the tiles are dried, grout, and then seal the grout according to the manufacturer's recommendations. (For grouting tips, see "Replace a Damaged Tile Section" on page 93.)

Replace a Three-Handle Tub/ Shower Faucet

WHAT YOU'LL NEED

Tub/shower faucet kit with valve

Screwdrivers

Drill/driver*

Mini pipe cutter

Copper pipe

Appropriate faucet fittings

Wire pipe brushes

Flux

Torch

Lead-free solder

Rag

Heat-resistant shield and gloves

Screws and cross-brace*

Teflon tape or thread sealant

* If applicable

If you're considering taking down your walls to replace your tub surround (see the previous project), it's the perfect time to update your tub/ shower faucet. This project is simplest when the walls are open, or if there's an access panel built into the other side of the tub wall. If this is not the case, you'll need to strategically open up that section of wall to access the faucet body.

CONSIDER THIS

When choosing a new tub/shower faucet, be sure to find one that matches your faucet's handle configuration.

You'll need to know how to sweat pipe for this project (see the sidebar "How to Sweat Pipe" on page 170).

This project addresses replacing the tub/shower faucet from an access panel.

Always follow the manufacturer's faucet installation instructions and safety recommendations.

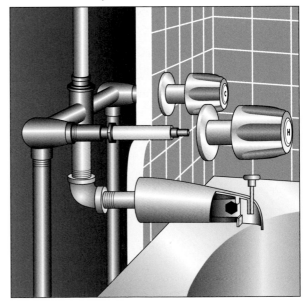

PREP WORK

- Shut off the water from the main or from a designated shut-off valve to this bathroom.

- Remove the old handles, tub spout, and showerhead. Handles usually have a screw beneath a decorative cap (a); once it's unscrewed, the handle will pull off. (Also, see "Replace a Showerhead" on page 83 and "Replace a Tub Spout" on page 91.)

- Open up the access panel to reveal the shower body and pipes. If there is cross-bracing (a piece of wood screwed between the studs to which the shower body is secured for proper bracing), carefully remove it.

- You'll need to cut out the old faucet body. These cuts will be made on each pipe that attaches to it at lengths that will enable you to solder on new pipes with fittings for the new faucet body. With a mini pipe cutter, cut the shower and tub-spout pipes as well as the hot and cold water supply pipes. To use the cutter, open its jaws so the pipe fits in its curve (b). Tighten the cutter onto the pipe. When it's snug, spin the cutter around the pipe. As the cutter wheel scores the pipe, gradually tighten it so it cuts deeper until it slices all the way through. **Note:** It may be easier to remove all of the tub-spout pipes and start fresh, especially if they're galvanized.

- Pull out the old faucet body.

THE PROJECT

1 Insert the new faucet body into the holes. Be sure to check that it's not upside down. There should be a label indicating orientation.

2 How your faucet body is designed will determine what kind of fittings you'll need to join the supply lines, shower riser, and tub filler pipe. Cut the new pipe to the length that will accommodate the section you removed plus the appropriate fitting (a). One end will be sweat to the existing lines using a copper coupling. The other end will be either screwed or soldered to the faucet body (b). **Note:** If soldering, be sure to open the valve stems (see "How to Sweat Pipe" on page 170). If the fitting is threaded, use Teflon tape or thread sealant. Dry-fit all these connections before soldering or sealing them in place.

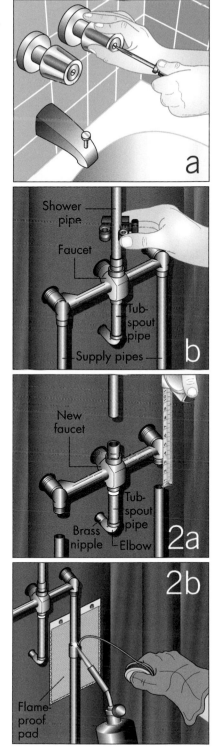

3 Once the lengths and connections are confirmed, join the new pipes to the faucet body permanently (screwing or sweating as necessary). Use a heat-resistant shield to protect the wall from the torch flame. **Note:** If cross-bracing is recommended by the faucet body manufacturer, screw the faucet body to the wood first, secure the wood to the studs, and then make your connection. (Of course, if you have access from the front, the cross-brace would go in first, and then the faucet body would be screwed to it.)

4 Turn on the water from the shut-off valves, and check for leaks.

5 Attach the tub spout, handles, and showerhead according to the manufacturer's instructions.

6 Close up the access panel.

Joining Galvanized Pipe to Copper Pipe

If you discover that your old pipes are galvanized, you'll need to use a special union to join them to your new copper pipes. This fitting is called a *dielectric union.* When unlike metals touch, they create corrosion that will eventually cause a leak. This special union joins the two pipes but separates them with a plastic sleeve and rubber washer.

To join the new copper pipe, turn off the water at the main and drain the system. With a hacksaw, cut the galvanized pipe a few inches from a joint. With a pipe wrench, unscrew this cut piece of pipe from the joint. Be careful not to wrench down or knock these pipes—it could cause a leak because of their age.

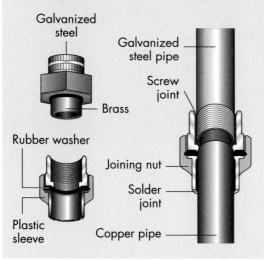

Insert a short galvanized *nipple* (a length of pipe threaded on both ends) and screw it into the old fitting—use pipe adhesive on the threads. Snug it with a wrench. Insert your copper length of pipe on the unthreaded side of the union and solder it in place. Screw the now joined copper pipe and union to the threaded galvanized nipple—use pipe adhesive on the threads.

Turn on the water and check for leaks.

If you find that the old galvanized pipe joint is clogged and heavily corroded or impossible to unscrew, your best bet is to call in a plumber who can better handle correcting a more intensive problem.

Toilets

It's your throne, why not install a new toilet that makes you feel like royalty?

Replace a Shut-off Valve

WHAT YOU'LL NEED

Replacement shut-off valve

Mini pipe cutter

2 tongue-and-groove pliers

Additional copper pipe and coupling—typically ½ inches*

Plumber's torch*

Handheld propane gas canister

Sandpaper*

Heat-resistant shield and gloves*

* If applicable

Often on older toilets, you'll go to shut off the water from the valve to start a toilet project and you're hit with a major roadblock—the valve leaks in the off position. Ugh! The only thing to do is replace it, because a leaky shut-off valve is the first sign of its failing completely, not to mention you can't get started on that toilet project.

If you live in an older home, I highly recommend inspecting all your shut-off valves (to your faucets, washing machine, and so on).

Go ahead and replace your shut-offs if

- Mineral deposits are built up along the valve.
- You shut a valve and it drips.
- You can't turn the handle at all because it's seized in the open position.

It's always better to install new shut-off valves when you're not *forced* to.

CONSIDER THIS

Replacing a shut-off valve requires that you shut off water to the house from the water main. After you remove that valve, it must be replaced or capped in order for water to be restored to the house.

Examine your existing shut-off valve. Is it copper pipe or galvanized? Is it a straight-stop or angle-stop (the threaded outlet is at a 90-degree angle to the toilet)? Is it soldered on or is it a compression fitting? You must know all these details in order to purchase the proper replacement.

Sometimes it's best to take the old shut-off valve with you to the store, but again, remember that the water main will have to remain off until you cap or replace the valve.

This project shows installing a ¼-turn angle-stop compression-type shut-off valve onto a copper stub-out.

PREP WORK

- Shut off the water from the water main.
- Drain the system by opening a faucet at a fixture above the shut-off and at the lowest point of the house.
- Disconnect the supply line to the toilet.

How do you level a toilet on an unlevel floor?

If, when installing a new toilet, you find you can't properly level it because of an unlevel floor, there are a couple ways to set things straight (pardon the corny pun).

    If you're installing the toilet on a *cement slab or plywood subfloor,* use a trowel-grade patching compound such as ARDEX Feather Finish. If you're going over plywood, be sure to check that the product you choose is designed to do so. Follow proper subfloor preparation as described by the manufacturer.

    If you're installing a toilet over a finished floor, or your existing toilet leans or rocks, you can use small plastic shims to make up for the surface variance around your bowl.

TO REMOVE A SOLDERED SHUT-OFF

- If you have extra pipe to spare on the stub-out, you can simply cut off the old valve with a pipe cutter. To use the cutter, open its jaws so the pipe fits in its curve. Tighten the cutter onto the pipe as close to the old valve as possible. When it's snug, spin the cutter around the pipe. As the cutter wheel scores the pipe, gradually tighten it so it cuts deeper, until it slices all the way through.

- If you don't have any extra pipe, you'll need to pull off the existing valve from the pipe. With a torch, heat the joint with the valve in the open position. When the solder begins to melt, wiggle off the old valve with pliers (a). Be sure to wear gloves and use a heat-resistant shield to protect the wall. Clean off any excess solder with sandpaper and wipe the pipe clean.

TO REMOVE A COMPRESSION SHUT-OFF

- Using two tongue-and-groove pliers, hold back on the stub-out or valve with one pair of pliers and unscrew the compression nut with the other pair of pliers. Unscrewing the valve will require a lot of elbow grease; however, be careful not to wrench so hard that you loosen a fitting behind the wall. When it's unscrewed, you'll find a brass ring (known as a *ferrule*) embedded onto the pipe (b). Leave this there along with the nut to use with the new compression valve. Skip to Step 2.

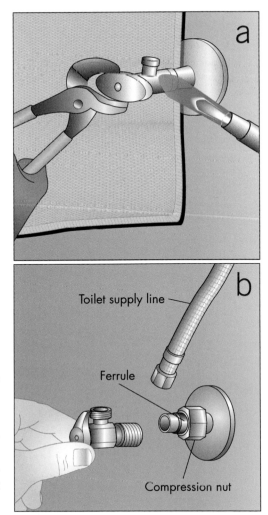

Toilet supply line

Ferrule

Compression nut

THE PROJECT

1 Slide the compression nut, and then the ferrule, onto the bare stub-out. Slide the valve onto the pipe until it stops. Rotate the valve on the pipe so that the outlet faces the right direction for the toilet.

2 Slide the compression nut back down toward the threads of the valve, wedging the ferrule in between it and the valve. **Note:** Don't use Teflon tape or thread adhesive with compression fittings. With two pairs of tongue-and-groove pliers, hold the valve in place and firmly tighten down the nut.

3 Make sure the valve is in the off position. Turn on the water at the main and check the valve for leaks. **Note:** If using the existing ferrule, it may no longer be able to create a seal. You'll know as soon as the water is turned on. If this is the case, you'll need to cut off that end of pipe because it'll be next to impossible to remove the old ferrule. If there is not enough pipe left on the stub-out, you'll need to sweat on a short length of pipe with a coupling. Reconnect the toilet supply line. Turn the new valve on and check for leaks.

How to Sweat Pipe

I know that the name may conjure an image of pipe "sweating" from condensation, but *sweat pipe* is actually a plumbing term used to describe joining copper pipes and fittings together with solder and a torch. As the solder melts around the pipe, it drips as if it were sweating—hence, the name.

When a pipe needs to be lengthened or a fitting (such as an elbow) is needed to configure the direction of a water line, copper fittings are soldered at each joint, which creates a watertight seal.

The process is simple, but it does take some practice. Also, because flame is used, you must take safety precautions. Keep in mind that if you're soldering next to any type of adjoining surface (such as a stud or wall), you need to use a heat-resistant shield to protect it. Be careful not to touch the pipe with your bare hands while it's still hot—use heat-resistant gloves. Use the following steps to sweat pipe:

1. Pipes will not solder if water is in the line. Drain any water from the pipe before getting started.
2. If you're soldering near a valve, put it in the open position before heating the pipe.
3. If you have cut pipe, ream the cut end—insert the short blade of the reamer tool into the pipe and firmly give it a few solid turns to remove any burs.
4. While wearing gloves, clean the ends of the pipe and fitting that will be mated to one another with a specialized wire brush and sandpaper.
5. Brush plumbing flux around the abraded surfaces, and join the pipe and fitting.
6. Pull out several inches of solder from its spool.
7. Heat the center of the fitting with the torch—moving the flame around it.
8. Just when the flux begins to smoke, move the flame away and press the tip of the solder onto the joint—it will instantly melt and wick into the joint. Touch the solder to the opposing side of the pipe so solder finds its way all the way around the pipe.
9. While the joint is still hot, brush some flux over the joint, and then give it a quick wipe with a damp rag.

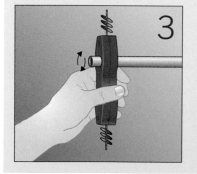

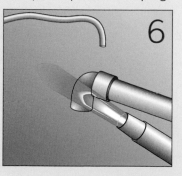

DVD Install a New Toilet

WHAT YOU'LL NEED

New toilet and seat

Flat head and Phillips screwdrivers

Tongue-and-groove pliers

Adjustable wrench

Utility knife

Mini hacksaw

New water supply line

Level

Wax ring or wax-free toilet seal (see the sidebar "Unexplained odor in your bathroom?" on page 173)

Scraper

Closet bolts

Penetrating oil

Plumber's putty

Large piece of cardboard or rug

Bucket

Large synthetic sponge

Gloves

Rag

Upgrading a toilet for comfort, better water conservation, more stylish design, or because it's just plain broken makes installing a new toilet a highly popular project.

Do your research before purchasing a new toilet and check to see if the manufacturer provides a flush performance rating. (Don't you hate it when you have to double-flush?)

CONSIDER THIS

A toilet is heavy. It's best to do this project with a partner. Be sure to bend at the knees when lifting.

Before starting this project, check to see that the shut-off valve is working properly (see "Replace a Shut-off Valve" on page 168).

PREP WORK

- Before removing the toilet, shut off the water at the shut-off valve.

- Flush the toilet a couple of times, and then sponge out any remaining water from the bowl and tank.

- Disconnect the water supply line to the toilet.

- If your toilet is in two parts (separate bowl and tank), remove the tank by unscrewing the two bolts in the tank—penetrating oil will help with the rust. Remove the tank from the bowl (a).

- To remove the bowl, lift off the decorative caps and unscrew the closet bolts at the base (b). You may need to break a caulk seal around the base of the bowl with a utility knife. Carefully lift up the bowl.

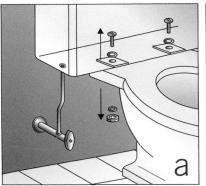

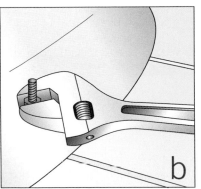

- Scrape away the old wax ring so that the flange is smooth.
- Plug the drain with a large rag (shown in the illustration) to prevent sewer gases from wafting into the room (c). Pull out the old closet bolts.

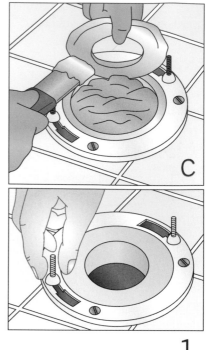

THE PROJECT

INSTALL THE BOWL

1 Insert the new closet bolts in the flange. Make sure they're properly centered.

2 Remove the rag from the drain. Press the wax ring down onto the flange. Or, for the wax-free toilet seal, press the adhesive side of the seal onto the outlet horn under the toilet.

3 Turn the bowl carefully upside down onto a protective piece of cardboard or rug. Apply a bead of plumber's putty on the base of the toilet where it will meet the floor. (See the sidebar "Plumber's Putty" on page 128.)

4 Carefully lift the toilet, center it over the flange, visually line up the bolt holes to the closet bolts, and guide the bowl down onto the flange. Press the bowl straight down, applying even pressure so the bowl compresses the wax ring. Do not twist the bowl.

5 Screw the nuts onto the closet bolts. Do not over-tighten—doing so will crack the porcelain. Alternate tightening down each bolt until they're both snug. Snap on the caps. If the bolts are too long, you may need to cut them with a mini hacksaw.

INSTALL THE TANK

6 Carefully turn over the tank onto a protective surface and slip on the rubber gasket (tank-to-bowl washer) around the tank's outlet hole.

7 Lift up the tank over the bowl, visually align the bolt holes, and set the tank onto the bowl.

8 Insert the tank bolts with rubber washers attached and tighten the nuts from underneath. Alternate tightening down each bolt until they're both semi-snug.

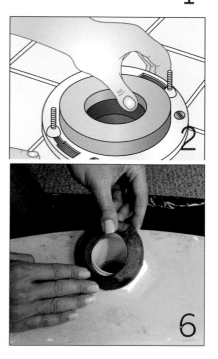

9 Check for level. With a level on the tank, tighten down the bolts, keeping an eye on the bubble for level. For the final snug turns, don't spin the bolt from the top; instead, hold back the bolt with a screwdriver and tighten strictly from the nut so as not to disturb that rubber washer seal. Be careful not to over-tighten. **Note:** If you're having difficulty leveling the toilet, see the sidebar "How do you level a toilet on an unlevel floor?" on page 169.

10 Connect the water supply line. Check that all the parts in the tank from the factory are tightened down.

11 Turn on the shut-off valve and check for leaks at the valve and all toilet connections.

12 Adjust the tank fill level. Look for a fill mark and use the adjustment screw on the fill valve to set the proper fill height.

13 Flush the bowl and make sure it's all working properly.

14 Put on the tank lid. Attach the toilet seat.

15 Wipe away any putty that squeezed out at the base.

Unexplained odor in your bathroom?

It's probably a problem with the wax ring—also known as a *Johnny ring.* The wax ring that sits between your toilet's flange and drain pipe has two very important functions: It stops liquid and waste from leaking out under your toilet base when you flush and prevents sewer gases from seeping up the drain and into your home. This is an awful lot to expect from a little wax ring.

Wax rings have been around forever and work great—that is, until they stop working. If the toilet  wasn't well seated over the wax ring, the seal is sure to fail in no time. A way to avoid this problem completely is not to use any wax at all.

Fernco Wax Free Toilet Seal creates a tight seal and takes away any guesswork out of the installation. It sticks to the bottom of the bowl, creating one seal, and then actually sits down into the drain pipe, creating a second positive seal.

So if there's a mystery odor in your bathroom, do a little sniffing around your toilet base. If the odor is coming from there, install a Fernco Wax Free Toilet Seal. In fact, it's a smart choice for new toilet installations as well. *Sorry, Johnny.*

Walls and Floors

New tiles for the toes and exhaust fan for the nose. Projects like these are a sure way to please all your senses the moment you step foot into your bathroom.

Tile a Floor

WHAT YOU'LL NEED

Floor tiles

Adjustable wrench

Flathead and Phillips screwdrivers

Drill/driver

Nippers

Hammer or mallet

Utility knife

Floor scraper

Metal putty knife

Rod saw

Heat gun*

Manual or wet blade tile cutter

Rag

Tape measure

Pencil and marker

¼-inch cement backer board

Backer board cutter

Framing square

Chalk line

Painter's tape

Continued on next page

Ceramic tile is, hands down, the classic floor choice for bathrooms. With its durability in wet environments, its affordability, and its limitless style selections, no wonder it's such a favorite. Additionally, do-it-yourselfers thrive with user-friendly tile-cutting tools on the market today—like a portable wet tile saw, which make cutting numerous tiles a breeze.

CONSIDER THIS

To achieve a successful tile job, you must have a sound sub-floor and underlayment. Any unstable or uneven surface will ruin a new tile installation.

You'll want to lay tile under the toilet, so removing the bowl will be necessary.

Generally, it takes 24 hours before you can walk on newly installed tile, and 72 hours before allowing heavy traffic. Check manufacturer's instructions and drying times.

Be sure to choose tiles that are specifically made for floors. (Typically, wall tile will not be dense enough to hold up for flooring.)

To calculate how much tile to purchase, determine the square footage (length × width), and then add 10 percent of that number to the total. Tile boxes will tell you the number of tiles and square footage they will cover.

You may need to cut the bottom of the bathroom door to accommodate the new height of the finished floor.

You'll need to choose a threshold that will transition your bathroom tile to whatever type of flooring is on the other side of the door. The threshold could be wood or marble, but most importantly it must be able to accommodate the two types of flooring.

This project addresses removing a vinyl tile floor from a plywood subfloor, installing a ¼-inch cement backer board underlayment, and then laying ceramic tile as seen in the cross-section on the left.

WHAT YOU'LL NEED

Continued from previous page

Noncorrosive counter sinking screws

Tile spacers

Nippers

Earplugs, mask, safety glasses

Alkali-resistant fiberglass tape

4-foot level

Abrasion stone

Bedding block (length of two-by-four)

Grouting supplies (grout, rubber float, large synthetic sponge, bucket of water, clean rag)

Grout sealer

Threshold transition

One-by furring strips

Modified thin-set mortar

Notched trowel

Compass*

Cardboard*

PREP WORK

- Remove the toilet and plug the drain hole with a rag (see "Install a New Toilet" on page 171).

- Remove any *shoe molding*—the rounded strip of molding that finishes and protects the baseboard. (If there is only baseboard molding, plan to add shoe molding that will create a finished look.)

- Remove the old vinyl tile using a floor scraper. For stubborn tile, a heat gun is useful to loosen the adhesive (a).

- Make sure plywood subfloor is sound and flat. Replace any damaged sections.

- Clean away all loose debris.

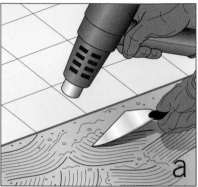

THE PROJECT

INSTALL ¼-INCH CEMENT BACKER BOARD

1 Determine the layout of the cement board by aligning boards perpendicular to the subfloor joints. Be sure to stagger all of the joints. Allow a ⅛-inch gap between cement board edges, walls, and cabinets. Score and snap boards as you would drywall.

2 Trowel a ¼-inch layer of modified thin-set onto the subfloor. Embed the boards into the wet mortar.

3 Screw the boards in place, every 8 inches with appropriate screws. Be sure screws are flush with the surface. Do not fasten screws ⅜ inch from board edges or 2 inches from the corner (to avoid cracking).

4 Prefill joints with the same thin-set, and then embed alkali-resistant fiberglass tape and smooth down and seal the joints with an additional pass of mortar. Allow the mortar to dry completely before tiling.

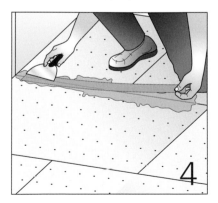

DETERMINE CERAMIC TILE LAYOUT

5 You'll need to establish a starting course of tile. Between the two most prominent walls, dry-fit tiles using spacers. Your goal is to end up with the following criteria for optimum results:

- Full tiles at the door and along the shower/tub.
- Equal-size tiles along the walls that face one another.
- No sliver-size tiles. Avoid a layout that creates a course of tiles that needs to be smaller than 2 inches.

No matter how experienced you are at tiling, it's likely that you won't be able to achieve all of these criteria and some choices will need to be made. Keep in mind the big picture of the floor. For example, tiles running along the toe-kick of a cabinet base aren't very noticeable.

6 Once the first course of tiles is determined, dry-fit a second perpendicular course at the center of this row. See if this produces an acceptable layout according to the criteria listed above. Adjust one or both of the rows if necessary.

7 Line up a framing square on top of one corner of the tile intersection; mark a right angle on the floor. Remove the tiles.

8 To establish your work lines, use one leg of the marked right angle to snap a chalk line from one wall to the other. Snap a second line to the opposite walls using the other leg of the right angle. Check for square using the 3-4-5 method (see "Establishing 'Square' with the 3-4-5 Triangle Method" on page 180). (This step is particularly important for larger floors where going even slightly off square will be cumulative over long tile courses, resulting in a sloppy looking tile job.)

9 Because it'll be hard to see the chalk line as you apply the mortar, screw down two straightedges (one-by furring strips work well) that will act as guidelines creating a quadrant to tile in. Put painter's tape on their edges to prevent mortar from sticking to them.

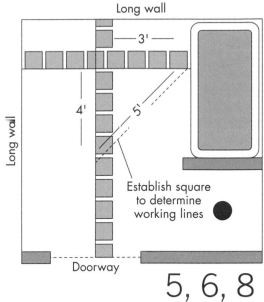

Long wall

— 3' —

4'   5'

Long wall

Establish square to determine working lines

Doorway

5, 6, 8

LAY THE TILE

10 Apply mortar with a notched trowel in a square slightly larger than a few rows of tile.

11 First, use the straightedges to lay out the tiles, and then use the tile edges to continue keeping uniform joints.

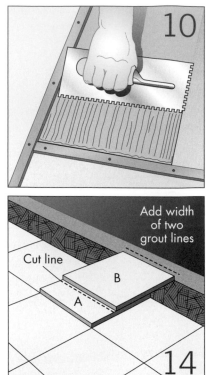

- Be sure to use tile spacers in between each tile unless tiles have built in nubs.
- Use the butt of your palm to embed tiles in the mortar.
- Slide a bedding block over the tiles and tap with a hammer or mallet to uniformly pound them down in place.
- Check the tile surface regularly with a level.
- If a tile sinks, pry it up and add mortar beneath it.
- Clean out any mortar that may squeeze up through the joints.
- Keep using the framing square to check that your rows are square.
- Continue to lay out all the full tiles in this quadrant. We'll leave all cut tiles for the end.

12 Unscrew the straightedges and rescrew one of them along one of the remaining chalk lines. Continue to spread mortar and lay all full tiles in this section.

13 Repeat the above step with the remaining chalk line until all the full tiles (also called *field tiles*) are set.

14 After the full tiles are dry, come back and lay all the cut tiles.

- To cut a **straight border** tile (the tile that borders a wall or cabinet), do the following to transfer the border measurement onto the tile: Lay a tile exactly over the adjoining full tile (tile A). Lay another tile over that tile, but line it up so that it rests over the border space (tile B) leaving the width of two joints away from the wall or cabinet. Use this tile to mark a line across the tile beneath it. Take the marked tile and cut it.
- To cut an **outside corner,** follow the preceding step twice—once on each side of the corner. This will create an L shape to be cut out that will fit that corner perfectly.
- Cut all the border tiles in a run first, number them (just in case the wall or cabinet isn't square), and then lay them in that order. Always do a dry fit first.
- For **odd-shaped cuts,** use a compass to transfer the shape onto the tile, or use cardboard to cut a template, and then trace the shape onto the tile.

15 Once all the tile is dry, grout the entire floor. (For grouting tips, see "Replace a Damaged Tile Section" on page 93.)

16 After the grout has dried for 48 to 72 hours, seal the grout joints with a penetrating sealer. Follow the manufacturer's instructions and safety precautions.

17 Replace baseboard molding and install shoe molding.

18 Install the threshold transition.

19 Reinstall the toilet.

More Tile Tips

- Use a rod saw and nippers for curves and small cuts. Make the larger cuts first; then make finer cuts with these tools.
- If the rod saw itself doesn't fit in the opening that needs to be cut, unscrew one side of the blade, fit it in the opening, and refasten the blade.
- Don't let mortar sit for more than 10 minutes without laying tile on it. If it starts to dry, scrape it off and reapply.
- If you finish a section, scrape away any remaining mortar.
- Don't walk on tile for 24 hours after it's been installed.
- It's recommended to avoid heavy traffic for 72 hours after tile installation.

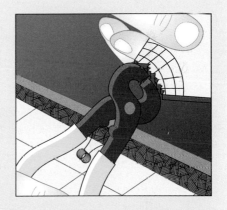

Establishing "Square" with the 3-4-5 Triangle Method

This method is used when needing to establish a right angle from two lines. The rule is, if you measure out 3 feet on one line, and then 4 feet on the other, the diagonal line that would join those two points will equal 5 feet, but only when that angle is at exactly 90 degrees.

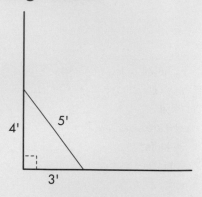

When using this method, you'll mark 3 feet and 4 feet on the given lines, and then adjust the angle they create, checking to see when you hit a 5-foot diagonal.

This method is best performed by two people, each using a tape measure to layout the two lines with a third tape measure to check for the 5-foot diagonal. Just be sure you're both measuring from the same side of the tape measure or the measurements will be off by the width of the tape. Once square is established, chalk lines may be snapped to create accurate working lines.

If we're going to get technical, it's actually the *Pythagorean theorem*—$a^2 + b^2 = c^2$, where *a* and *b* are the sides creating the right angle, and *c* is the diagonal line facing the right angle (a.k.a., the *hypotenuse*). (In this case, $3^2 + 4^2 = 5^2$, or $9 + 16 = 25$.)

Who knew back in high school that you'd end up using all that seemingly useless math to lay tile in your bathroom?

Install an Exhaust Fan

WHAT YOU'LL NEED

Combination exhaust fan/light

Flathead and Phillips screwdrivers

Stud finder

Drywall knife (jab saw)

Utility knife*

Straightedge

Drill/driver

4-inch hole saw

Pencil

Tape measure

Safety glasses

Foiled duct tape

1½-inch drywall screws

1½-inch stainless-steel screws

Flexible duct wall vent kit (check exhaust fan manufacturer's recommendation for duct type)

Extension ladder

Exterior-grade silicone caulking

Non-contact voltage tester

Electric cable connector

Wire nuts

Foam rubber*

*If applicable

Getting rid of moisture in the bathroom should be the number-one motivation for installing an exhaust fan—and not just because it makes your hair frizz when you're trying to blow-dry it. Moisture causes all kinds of ugliness—mold and mildew, blistering paint, foggy mirrors, foul odors, and so on.

Today combination exhaust fan/lights are so attractive and quiet, you'd never even know they have an exhaust. Because the wiring and switch are already there, replacing a standard ceiling fixture with this type of exhaust makes the installation very easy.

CONSIDER THIS

There are two ratings that need to be considered when choosing an exhaust fan—cubic feet per minute (CFM) and sone.

CFM represents how many times the fan can exchange the bathroom air in an hour: the higher the CFM, the more powerful the fan. This number is relative to the cubic feet (volume) of the space. To calculate the proper CFM, use this equation: volume ÷ 7.5. For example, if the bathroom's volume is 800 (10 feet in length × 10 feet in width × 8 feet in height), the CFM would be 106.7 (800 ÷ 7.5 = 106.7). So a fan with a CFM of 107 or greater will be the proper size fan for that space.

The *sone* is a unit of perceived loudness—the lower the sone, the quieter the fan. Obviously, quieter is preferable, but generally, the quieter the costlier. Just as a point of reference, a refrigerator has a sone of 1.0. Generally, fans can range from less than 1.0 to 4.0 sones.

An exhaust fan must always vent to the exterior. Venting solely up to the attic is not acceptable.

Fans may vent up through the ceiling and out the roof or through an exterior wall.

Installing an exhaust with an integrated light can be used to replace a ceiling fixture and allow you to use the existing electric supply to avoid having to run a separate line to it.

This project addresses replacing the existing ceiling fixture with a combination ceiling exhaust fan/light that vents through the ceiling, into the attic, and then out an exterior wall with siding.

Installation of exhaust fans vary depending on brand. Always follow the manufacturer's instructions and safety precautions.

With any fan, be sure to check that the distance from your existing light fixture to the exterior wall does not exceed the maximum duct run as determined by the manufacturer.

PREP WORK

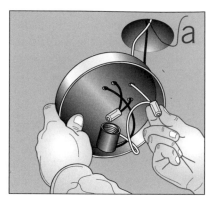

- To remove the old light fixture, first shut the power off to the light from the service panel.

- Removing the old fixture will vary depending on what type of light you have. Generally, you'll first need to remove the globe or light cover, and then the bulbs.

- After the globe and bulb(s) are removed, there may be nuts that secure the fixture base to the ceiling (a). Unscrew them and pull the fixture away from the ceiling. If it has been caulked or painted, it may help to run a utility knife around the seam where the fixture meets the ceiling (being careful not to damage the drywall).

- Pulling out the fixture should reveal wires, an electrical box, and potentially a round mounting plate or strap. Mentally note how the wires are connected (usually black to black, white to white, ground to ground [copper or green]), because you'll need to repeat the same wiring.

- With a non-contact voltage tester, test that the power is off. Hold the tester up to the wires. No light or ringing indicates no power.

- Unscrew the wire nuts and disconnect the fixture. Set the fixture aside. It's good practice to reconnect the wire nuts to the now single wires.

- If there's a mounting plate that's similar to the new one, you may leave the old one in place. If not, remove it.

- A bare copper ground wire may be screwed to the inside of the electrical box—disconnect it.

- You should now have a black, white, and ground wire coming out of your electric box.

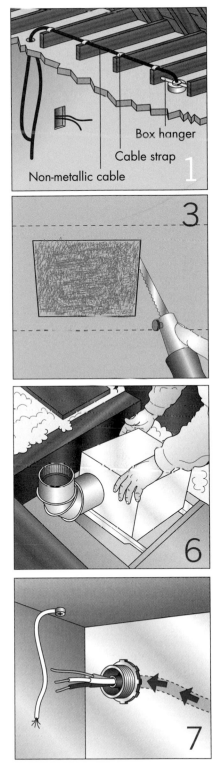

Box hanger

Cable strap

Non-metallic cable

THE PROJECT

SECURE THE HOUSING TO THE JOISTS

1 From the attic, clear away any insulation. Remove the electric box from the joist and disconnect the cable from the box. This electric supply will be used to wire the fan.

2 From the bathroom, mark the joists on the ceiling. Place the exhaust housing or template over the opening so that it's positioned between the two joists. Make sure it's square, and then trace it on the ceiling. Make sure there will be clearance from the joists to attach a duct connector/elbow. (Depending on the model, you may have to remove the blower/motor from the housing.)

3 With a drywall saw, cut out the opening. Always wear safety glasses especially when working overhead.

4 Back in the attic, attach the duct connector/damper to the fan housing. Make sure that it's aiming straight up. Tape it with foiled duct tape.

5 Attach the cable connector to the housing. There will probably be a knockout that needs to be removed.

6 Set the housing down between the joists so that it sits perfectly centered and flush to the ceiling opening. Screw the housing to the joists. There may be mounting tabs/holes in the unit to do this, or you may need to purchase additional hanger bars.

CONNECT THE ELECTRIC CABLE AND VENT

7 Feed the electric cable through the connector that you've attached to the housing, and then tighten the connector so the cable is snug.

8 Attach the flexible vent hose to the duct connector/elbow and duct-tape the joint. Check the manufacturer's instructions to see if insulation may come in direct contact with the vent.

9 Select the closest route from the exhaust to the attic wall and select a spot to make the vent opening. Drill a pilot hole in the center of that spot.

10 From the exterior of the house, locate the hole you just made. Using a 4-inch hole saw, use that drill hole as the center and drill the vent hole. (Be careful working from an extension ladder and make sure that it's properly positioned by the hole so you don't have to stretch in order to reach it.)

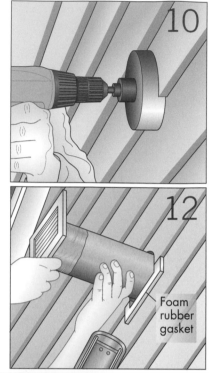

11 Attach the metal duct to the louvered vent. Secure it with duct tape.

12 Slide the vent through the opening and fasten it to the wall with stainless-steel screws. Apply an exterior-grade bead of silicone caulk around the vent to create a waterproof seal. If the vent plate does not sit flush to the wall because of siding, cut a foam-rubber gasket to fill in any gaps.

Foam rubber gasket

13 Back in the attic, attach the metal duct to the end of the flexible vent hose. Secure it with duct tape.

14 Make sure any insulation is properly replaced. Check with the manufacturer to see if insulation may come in direct contact with the housing or duct.

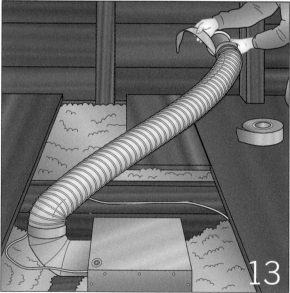

MAKE THE WIRE CONNECTIONS

15 Recheck that the power is still off to the supply cable with an electric tester.

16 You'll need to expose the wires of the unit. Typically, there will be a wire receptacle you'll unscrew in the housing.

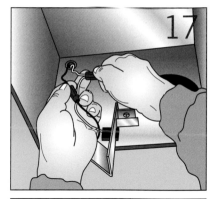

17 Connect the black to black and white to white with wire nuts. Screw the ground to a green grounding screw in the housing. Always check the unit's wiring schematic provided by the manufacturer.

18 Gently fold the wires back into the receptacle and screw it closed.

19 Plug the blower into the receptacle. There will be some kind of quick-connect wire harness to plug into. (First, reinstall the blower/motor if you had to remove it to free the housing.)

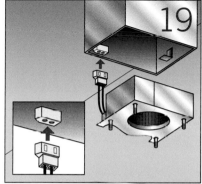

20 Test that the blower is working. Restore power to the switch and turn on the unit.

21 Confirm that the blower is working properly by holding a strip of tissue near the blower (but not so close that it touches the fan). See if it draws the tissue toward it.

22 Turn off the switch.

COMPLETE INSTALLATION

23 Plug the light assembly (grill) into the indicated quick-connect plug.

24 Fasten the lighting mount onto the housing on the ceiling.

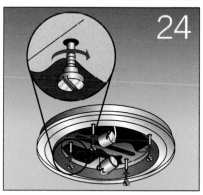

25 Install the light bulbs and secure the glass dome.

26 Turn on the switch. Confirm that the light and blower are working. Excellent work!

Part 4

Total Indulgence: Dreaming up the Perfect Bathroom

Footprint and Layout:
What Works for You

Consider the human face. How many trillions of versions are there of it? Yet the formula is always the same—two eyes, one nose, and one mouth. Astounding! I can't help but ponder a similar formula when I look at a bathroom. The standard bathroom is divided into four quarters that relate to fixtures—one toilet, one sink, one shower, and one tub. So simple, yet the possibilities are endless.

Exploring the Possibilities

What an exciting prospect when you're at the point of tearing out your entire bathroom and starting from scratch. (I'd say it can be downright intimidating when you consider the quarter million years of genetics that went into creating faces!)

In design, *layout* describes placement of these fixtures, while the *footprint* describes the configuration of the walls that surround them. No matter what the size or shape of your bathroom, there are three principles that must always be considered when designing a bathroom:

- **Inherent space characteristics.** Examples would be window placement, ceiling height, soffits, radiator, and so on.

- **Standardized space guidelines.** These measurements were established to ensure a person's comfort and safety when performing all bathroom functions. Space guidelines exist for every room in a house. Always check local building codes before planning a remodel.

- **Flow and functionality.** These elements speak to how the entire space moves and performs relative to each fixture. For example, is the towel rack conveniently placed near the shower or the tissue holder near the toilet? Is there adequate storage surface around the sink?

The best way to experiment with layout is to sketch the space on graph paper, using each square to represent a unit of measurement, say each square equals 3 inches, so 4 squares equal a foot. Be sure to mark not only existing room dimensions, but all fixtures and features of the space—door swing, windows, outlets, etc.

Now ask yourself, what works in the space, what doesn't? Where are the traffic jams? What are the inconveniences? Think about bathrooms you've been in that have really rocked your world—what was it about them that made navigating through them such a pleasure?

Survey what rooms share common walls to the bathroom and consider where logical footprint changes can be made. For example, does the existing shower stall share the wall with a closet? That would offer a perfect opportunity to bump the stall into that closet, opening up more space in the bathroom, with minimal effect on the adjoining room.

Always keep in mind that bigger is not necessarily better. Sometimes "big" just translates into time-consuming added steps in getting from Point A to Point B, with no real payoff. A small, well-appointed space is always more enjoyable to use than one that's unnecessarily large.

Master Bathroom

Typically, the master bath is the largest bathroom in a home, is adjacent to or incorporated within the master bedroom (making it a suite), and is designed for two. The concept of a master bath has become far more than a serviceable pit stop for a couple, but rather a retreat someone can escape to after a long day. With the nation's ever-growing love affair with spas, no wonder builders are investing so much money into master baths. If just looking at a luxurious bathroom can make a potential buyer go "Ahh . . . ," then the sale is halfway there. Today, the master bath is considered one of the most important amenities to a house.

When it comes to remodeling your master bath, you really need to make it all about you (and your partner). Sit down and ask yourself what you want from your bathroom, and be honest. What may look fabulous in a showroom may end up being something you'll never actually use—but it'll have cost you a fortune. For example, a popular feature in many new homes is a large soaking tub. To me, a long, hot bath is a gift from the gods, but to someone like my girlfriend Phyllis, a busy working mother of two, it's just something else she has to clean. "Who has time for a bath anyway?" I can just hear her.

To help define your true bath lifestyle, ask yourself these questions:

- Are my partner and I desperate to have more individualized his-and-her facilities?
- Would I prefer a semi-enclosed or totally separate toilet compartment?
- Should I consider a dedicated makeup/hair station?
- Would I prefer one large shower stall as opposed to a tub/shower?
- What is my daily bathroom routine?
- How much time do really I spend in my bathroom?
- Would I spend more time in it if the space were conducive for relaxing?
- What special features would I really love—sauna, high-tech toilet bidet, linen closet?

A common consideration in a master bath is how to create privacy for each person without having to lock out your partner. It's hard to relax in a tub if your partner barges in for a quick shower and shave. When exploring your master-bath footprint, consider dividing the space in a way to create a half bath (toilet and sink) in one section and bath and shower stall in another. The goal is to create a bathroom in which two people can simultaneously use the space comfortably.

Consider This for Luxury Master Baths

FOR SHOWERS
- A two-person stall with dual temperature controls for his-and-her settings
- Rejuvenating body sprays that target muscle groups
- Hand shower
- Seating area
- Enclosed steam shower

FOR SINKS
- Dual pedestal sinks with flanking linen tower cabinets
- A long double sink vanity or separate vanities
- Instead of side-by-side sinks, think of placement on opposite walls, or back-to-back in the center of the space or perpendicular to a wall

FOR BATHROOMS

Before you decide on a tub, make sure your water heater is large enough to fill it with hot water, or consider a tankless water heater. An inline heater will maintain tub temperature without having to add more water.

- A whirlpool tub
- A one- or two-person tub—just keep in mind that a two-person tub takes a lot more water, space, and time to fill.
- A soaking tub, which is deeper than a standard tub and ideal for sitting with water up to your shoulders

FOR TOILETS

- A remote-controlled high-tech toilet with built-in bidet
- A heated toilet seat, which is perfect for cold mornings
- An automatic toilet seat that lifts and lowers according to the user's intentions—no more touching the seat or "you forgot to put the seat down!"

Kids' Bathroom

Creating a fun and safe bathroom for kids should be an exercise in indulgence *and* restraint. You need to focus on creating something cool for kids, but you don't want to let your inner child run amok. What you'll likely end up with is an over-the-top, matchy-matchy, theme park-looking space that will quickly lose its novelty.

When remodeling a kid's bath, child-size vanities, cabinets, and fixtures (lower and with shorter arm reach) can be perfect for little tykes. That goes for accessories (towel rack, soap holders) and switch heights as well. However, a mini-me bathroom may not fare well for resale value. Ask yourself these questions before remodeling:

- How long do you plan on living in the house?
- How old is your child? Do you plan on having any more children?
- Will this bathroom be shared by adult guests?

Depending on how you answer these questions, you may realize that a combination of adult- and kid-size features may make more sense. For example, you can easily replace a smaller kid-size toilet when the child grows out of it. If you plan to move in a few years, maybe you're better off just adding kid-safe features and decorating for kids. Take time to make these decisions before going gaga over all the adorable kid-size fixtures available today.

I love the idea of having your child help choose the *theme* of the bathroom. Then it's up to you to make sure not every single article under the sun is purchased to match the theme. **Remember:** Overkill could be just one toilet seat cover away. Try to choose a theme that is somewhat evergreen—like Winnie the Pooh or beachscapes. What's hot at the moment could soon fade into oblivion, along with the décor of your bathroom.

Consider This for Kids' Baths

FOR SHOWER AND TUBS

- Grab rails to help them hold on while you're giving them a scrub-down
- No-skid bath mats or anti-slip porcelain tub treatment
- Decorative spout covers to prevent burns and bangs
- Anti-scald showerheads and tub spouts

FOR SINKS

- Specialized children's sinks offer a variety of fun shapes and colors—like a heart or a football. They're made from special solid-surface composite material that resists scratches and dents. The vanity opening will fit a standard drop-in sink, so if your child outgrows it, a new one can easily plop right in.
- A child's pedestal sink is the perfect height for a tot, meaning less chance for slipping and splashing. They take a standard rough-in, so upgrading to an adult size is possible.

FOR TOILETS:

- A child-size toilet makes going potty very easy because they need no assistance getting on and off the bowl. They take a standard 12-inch rough-in, so swapping out for an adult size would be easy.
- For standard toilets, allow extra room around it. The standard 30 inches (15 inches from the centerline of the bowl to any fixture, wall, or obstacle) will be tight for an adult to assist the child on the bowl.

Guest Bathroom

The name of the game for a guest bathroom is simple: Make your guests feel at home. No guest wants to snoop in cabinets and drawers for, say, toilet paper, so all bathroom necessities—towels, spare toothbrush, blow dryer, and so on—should be exposed and ready for the taking. Imagine how amenities are so beautifully displayed and at your disposal in a high-end hotel—that's what you should strive for in your guest bathroom. It's also important to provide adequate space for guests to be able to conveniently store their toiletry bags. You don't have to splurge on custom fixtures as you would in a master bath or powder room—simple and spacious is key in creating a comfortable space for your overnighters.

Consider This for a Guest Bath

- A built-in vanity with open storage for all bathroom necessities and sundries
- Conveniently placed open shelves for toiletry-bag storage
- Extra hooks for guests to be able to dry towels, bathing suits, and so on
- A dressing area and large mirror to allow guests to change in the bathroom comfortably and not have to parade around in a towel or robe

Wheelchair-Accessible Bathrooms

Barrier-free design (design that supports accessible living for individuals with disabilities) has given rise to a broader approach of space solutions called *universal design.* The concept of universal design embraces all people. In the past, "handicap" design meant sterile, institutional-looking amenities—far too unappealing and stigmatizing. Universal design has embraced the notion that good looks matter just as much as functionality.

Whether it's adults planning for a senior parent to move in or individuals anticipating recovering from surgery, trends show that people are more eager to opt for universal design when making bathroom choices.

Consider This for a Universal-Design Bath

FOR THE ROOM

- A wider bathroom door (at least 32 inches wide)
- An *expandable offset hinge* to the existing door, which will add 2 inches of clearance
- Lever-style handles on doors and cabinets
- Rocker panel light switches as opposed to toggle ones

- Non-slip flooring treatment
- A phone and intercom
- Ample clear floor space for a wheelchair
- Easy-access storage space and hooks

FOR THE SHOWER/TUB

- Grab bars
- Walk-in, low-curb threshold
- A seating area
- A handheld shower

- Lever-style, easily accessible controls
- No-skid bath mats or anti-slip porcelain tub treatment

FOR THE SINK

- Height of 32 inches
- Lever-style faucet controls

- Knee space under the sink
- An adjustable tilt mirror (see page 74)

FOR THE TOILET

- Height of 17 inches
- At least 42 inches of clear space next to the toilet

- Convenient toilet-paper access with simple roll-changing design

Design:

Creating the Ideal Look and Feel for Your Bathroom

Every element in your bathroom will define its look and feel. When you're dreaming up your perfect bathroom, you need to explore the plethora of exquisite materials and fixtures on the market today.

The first thing you should ask yourself is what kind of mood you want your bathroom to create the moment you step foot in it. Do you want fresh and uplifting, dreamy and romantic, playful and kitsch? Once you decide on the mood, keep that feeling in mind as you make your choices.

Where to Get Started

To help choose your bathroom's look and feel, try to experience various bath designs firsthand. For inspiration, browse home-and-garden shows, go to open houses, and visit bathroom showrooms where you can see various bathroom vignettes set up.

Because I travel a lot, I'm always eager to see what my hotel bathroom will have to offer. I can recall being so excited to stay in a chic boutique hotel, famous for its minimalist design. I was absolutely enamored by the looks of this place, but here's the funny thing: When I actually got to use the bathroom, I couldn't help but feel like someone in scrubs and a mask was about to walk in on me to perform a medical procedure! A little too sterile for my taste, but that's just me.

Design Options

The following are some basic design options that I've categorized to help you define the look and feel you want to create.

- **Contemporary.** Today often interchangeable with "modern" and "minimalist," contemporary bathroom designs are sleek, cool, and clean. Squared angles are common, curves are elongated, and structures are reduced to their simplest form. An example of this would be a sculptured one-piece toilet.

- **Nature inspired.** A mountain lodge, a serene waterfall, a rain forest—these designs pull from all the wondrous elements nature has to offer and uses many natural resources to do so. Natural stone, bamboo, grasses, and rough-sawn wood are common in these bathrooms. Because these qualities are inherently conducive to relaxation, they're a popular choice for spa-driven bathroom designs that seek to create a sanctuary-type atmosphere.

- **Old world.** This design style incorporates beauty from throughout the ages. Be it a French flare of velvet drapery and gilded sconces or the Byzantine-arched windows and mosaics of a Middle Ages cathedral, old-world bathrooms can really take you on a mini passage through time. A less period-intensive perspective of old world crosses into traditional design that draws anywhere from British colonial to French country.

- **Transitional.** A marriage of contemporary and traditional, this design offers the best of both worlds. It takes the stodginess out of traditional and the sterility out of contemporary. Here you can combine fresh and clean with warm and friendly. For example, modern fixtures can be paired with crackled subway tile.

Flooring

The number-one question to ask regarding bathroom flooring is whether it's impervious to water. Even if it's a powder room, bathroom floors get wet—whether from an overfilled sink, splashing kids, or sloppy toilet users. You want to be able to get it wet, mopped, and cleaned up without any worries.

The next two issues are durability and performance. If you spill nail polish, will it ruin the floor? Will it be very slippery when wet? How will it feel under your bare feet?

Last, but not least, style. How will the flooring you choose affect the look and feel of the space? Does it work with the mood you want to create?

The following explores some of the more popular and interesting flooring choices for bathrooms. As you browse through them, see which best meets these criteria.

Ceramic and Porcelain Tile

The most popular choice for bathrooms, these tiles are durable, easy to clean, won't absorb water or odors, and are hypoallergenic—they can't harbor mites and allergens. The array of colors, textures, and arrangements are endless. Choosing one may be overwhelming, but the beauty is, whatever you're dreaming up in your head is certain to be out there.

Ceramic tiles are rated by the Porcelain Enamel Institute (PEI). The scale goes from PEI-1 (no-traffic, wall use only) to PEI-5 (the most durable for high-traffic areas).

It's also important to know the difference between ceramic and porcelain tile. The formal distinction can get very technical, but to sum it up, porcelain tiles are generally denser (therefore, harder) and more impervious to water than ceramic tiles. Though both tiles are man-made from natural materials, porcelain tiles are fired under higher temperatures, which give them a higher impervious rating.

The following are some notable characteristics and distinctions between porcelain and ceramic tiles.

PORCELAIN TILES

- The clay body, or *bisque,* of the tile is lighter in color than ceramic tiles.
- They may be marked "Porcellanato," which means porcelain in Italian.
- Some may be *through-bodied,* which means they're the same color throughout and will have no glaze. This characteristic makes a chip almost unnoticeable.
- They may be glazed or unglazed; unglazed tiles offer more slip resistance.
- They're slightly more expensive than ceramic tiles.
- Because of their high density, they're hard to cut and bond.
- They're extremely well suited for high-traffic areas.

CERAMIC TILES

- The bisque is a dark-red terra-cotta color.
- They're typically glazed.
- They cut and bond more easily than porcelain tiles.
- You have the greatest array of choices with ceramic tiles.
- Although less dense than porcelain, some ceramic tiles can offer a PEI-4 rating, which is recommended for all residential applications.

Natural Stone

This genre of flooring includes travertine, marble, granite, slate, and limestone. The exquisiteness of these surfaces is undeniable, and so is the cost. Although it's one of the most expensive flooring options, its timeless beauty and durability certainly are rewarding. Keep in mind that even though they're durable, they require maintenance. I recommend that stone floors be sealed yearly. They should be cleaned with specialized stone products that won't strip away this seal or damage the surface. Water should not be left to sit, so wiping up after use should be common practice.

Stone can be tumbled, honed, or polished. Tumbled stone offers an imperfect and textured surface. Honed stone is smooth but has a dull finish. Polished stone is buffed to a high gloss. Each finish offers its own beauty and style, as well as drawbacks to be considered for a bathroom. For example, tumbled stone may feel too rough under foot, and polished stone is extremely slippery when wet.

Glass Tile

Iridescent, translucent, matte—no matter what the look, glass tiles bring a three-dimensional excitement to a floor that can't go unnoticed. Many glass tiles are made of 100 percent recycled glass, which make them environmentally appealing. Be sure to choose a tile that's suitable for flooring. Do-it-yourselfers should know that glass tile is definitely more finicky to cut than ceramic tile.

Hardwood

Some say wood and water don't mix, which would make hardwood floors a no-no for bathrooms. But how would that explain wooden boats, canoes, and kayaks? Which got me to thinking: Wood and water *do* mix as long the wood is properly installed, sealed, and cared for—just like the noble teak of a custom-built sailboat.

Hardwood floors are warm and inviting. There's something to be said for setting foot on a surface that won't send chills up your spine on a cold winter morning, the way ceramic tiles will. The various stains, plank sizes, and textures of woods offer a wide variety of choices that can fit easily into any bathroom design.

Whether they're dark, wide-planked, distressed or light, narrow-planked, and sleek, the following are some considerations that should always be adhered to when choosing and living with a hardwood bathroom floor:

- Only choose a hardwood—such as oak, maple, cherry, ash, or walnut. Unlike softwoods (such as spruce, fir, and pine), which more easily absorb ambient moisture, hardwood is resistant to damage and warping.

- Hardwood floors should be properly sealed with a polyurethane or polyacrylic. Penetrating seal and oil finish soaks won't provide enough protection from things like makeup stains and water spots.

- In very damp climates or bathrooms where excessive water splashes are inevitable, hardwood is not recommended.

- Spills on wood floors should be wiped up quickly.

- Regular cleaning is crucial to maintain the finish on wood floors.

If you love wood floors but are wary of the precautions that need to be taken with them in a bathroom, you may consider mixing flooring materials. For example, frame a section of tile simply around the bath/shower stall, but have hardwood running through the rest of the space.

Laminate

Laminate floors are distinguished by two characteristics: (1) They're floating, not nailed or glued to the subfloor, and (2) the plank face is made to look like a natural surface (say wood or stone), but is in fact a photo rendering atop multiple layers of mixed materials. Laminate floors are durable, affordable, water resistant, and easy to install.

Although many laminate floor manufacturers recommend their product for use in bathrooms, they always mention caveats that must be strictly adhered to when installing—like using a special sealant around the entire perimeter, all expansion spaces, and transitions. The fact is, if water seeps beneath the water-resistant surface through a failed seal or joint, the floor *will* buckle. Even if you wipe up the water immediately, if it gets under the surface, the damage is done. For this reason, I'd only recommend this type of flooring for half baths where no shower or tub means the risk from water damage would be at a minimum.

Engineered Hardwood

Typically, this floor has a top layer of hardwood over several layers of mixed wood and glue—the more layers, the more durable. They may be floating or nailed down like hardwood. In some respects, they're more stable than solid wood, but the same vulnerabilities that apply to laminate floors and hardwood floors also apply to engineered wood. The upside is they're less expensive than hardwood and the floating type are as easy to install as laminate floors.

Bamboo and Cork

Both renewable and sustainable materials, bamboo and cork flooring offer far more than an eco-friendly appeal. **Bamboo floor** is 25 percent harder than oak. Because it expands and contracts 50 percent less than hardwood, it can be used in high-humidity climates. However, planks could swell if water is left to stand, so wiping them down is a must. Vertical or horizontal grain pattern and natural or carbonized (darker) color offer a modest variety of looks to choose from.

Cork floors have more benefits and beauty than you could ever imagine. They're naturally stain, moisture, mold, and rot resistant. Although water is okay, flooding the floor is not. Ants and termites want nothing to do with cork, so although it's considered a wood, insect infestation is never a concern. It's hard to imagine that a material could be so flexible and durable at the same time—yet it is! It's warm, soft, and anti-skid—perfect for the tootsies. What will surprise you is the expansive variety of colors, patterns, and tile sizes on the market today. Installation is very simple. Maintenance is required, and manufacturers recommend using a finishing/sealant product every 9 to 12 months.

Carpet

Shocked that I would list carpet as a bathroom flooring option? Water-, stain-, mold-, and mildew-resistant carpets on the market today paired with the proper padding make carpet in bathrooms a desirable flooring option for individuals who are at high risk for slip-and-fall accidents. Though I don't recommend carpet for a high-traffic bathroom with splashing kids, it's ideal for, say, a senior couple who worries about taking a fall onto a hard surface like tile. (My mom enlightened me to this!)

Walls

How much visible wall space is there really in your bathroom? Mirrors, cabinets, shower stall, tub surround, and so on occupy much of the wall space in most bathrooms. For this reason, it's important to make what you do see of your walls really count.

Before deciding on a wall material, finish, or color, I ask myself what the intended purpose of the walls in this space is (other than holding up the ceiling)? Do I want them to act as a neutral backdrop for bold fixtures and cabinets? Do I want the color of the walls to set the overall mood of the room? Do I want a border tile to unite the entire space?

Play with questions such as these to help make your decisions, and don't be afraid to be adventurous. Years ago, I was appalled to learn that my girlfriend was having black-textured wallpaper installed in her windowless and miniscule powder room. As if that weren't dismal enough, all her fixtures were going to be *black*. I was sure that closing the door behind yourself would feel much like encasing yourself in a tomb. (Did I mention I'm claustrophobic?) Well, that wasn't the case at all. She installed a stunning polished-nickel ensemble—faucet, accessories, handles, and pulls. A large silver-scroll framed mirror hung over the sink, and overhead was an exquisite antique crystal chandelier. The space was gorgeous.

Design Options

Tile is a natural wall option in a bathroom, but it can quickly become excessive throughout the entire space, not to mention create an echo chamber. Consider some of these tile designs:

- One accent tiled wall where you can indulge in exotic tiles or mosaics
- Half-tiled walls finished with an exciting border tile
- Accent tiles of glass or metal randomly strewn throughout the tiled wall

Paint has limitless options in color and design. Painting techniques such as faux finishes and glazing will bring added visual interest to a bare wall. High-contrast color molding creates dimension in the space. A stencil or *trompe l'oeil* can be used to accent an interesting architectural feature like around a vaulted window.

Know that bathrooms are hard on painted walls. Especially if you have a high-traffic bathroom, be sure to choose a paint that's formulated to be washable and resistant to moisture and mildew. Generally, a paint that has a smooth and shiny surface is less able to hold in moisture and grime and performs better in busy bathrooms.

Wainscot and bead-board panels range from simple to stately. It can make a bathroom seems like it's part of a beach cottage or a turn-of-the-century mansion. My only reservation is that around water, special care needs to be taken with any wood materials.

Wallpaper is one wall material that I do *not* recommend in a full or half bath. I've been on too many jobs where taking down peeling moldy wallpaper was accompanied by homeowners swearing that they'd never put up paper again.

Cabinetry

For me, nothing screams opulence like custom cabinetry (or a custom vanity). There are so many aspects of cabinetry to consider—be prepared to spend an inordinate amount of time making your choices, and rightly so. Cabinetry can end up being the costliest aspect of your bathroom as well as provide the biggest impact.

Design Options

Here are some basic cabinetry features and topics you'll need to consider:

- **Layout.** What will work best in that particular space given its dimensions, and who will be using it? If there's ever a time to work with a professional designer, now would be it.

- **Wood characteristics.** Every wood has its own signature and, of course, price. For example, maple is characterized by its smooth and even grain, whereas pecan is known for its dramatic color variations. Walnut runs about twice the price of, say, white oak.

- **Finish.** Stains will enhance the wood grain, opaques provide a solid-body color, and glazes highlight deep crevices or all visible cabinet parts. Distressed techniques provide a vintage warmth and charm. No matter what the finish, it must be able to protect the wood and wipe up easily with a damp cloth.

- **Door styles and pulls.** Proportions, shapes, and details all need to be considered, especially since doors and pulls are such a prominent part of the look of the cabinets.

- **Quality.** Cabinets should be solid wood construction and hardwood framed. Hardware, guides, and joints should all be top quality. Smooth operation of drawers is a must. Check to see if the manufacturer offers a limited lifetime warranty.

Fixtures, Faucets, and Accessories

These elements are the real nuts and bolts of a bathroom. Every one of them is used hands-on every day—flushed, turned, pulled, drained, and so on. Whatever your design choice, be sure that they're durable, high quality, and installed properly.

Design Options

There are several ways to go about choosing fixtures, faucets, and accessories. Here are a couple of methods to help guide you through your quest:

- **Browse manufacturers' suites, collections, and ensembles.** For example, look for a matching toilet, sink/vanity, tub, and sometimes even furniture. Because everything is based around a common design, the guesswork is taken out of the equation. All you have to do is find a collection, color, and finish that fulfill your dream bathroom.

- **Choose unique pieces individually.** In this strategy, nothing matches, but the articles work together harmoniously. For example, you could feature a Venetian-glass mosaic sink, with an antique claw-foot tub—each featuring a different style faucet. This method takes a little more legwork, but there's something to be said for falling in love with each fixture after an onerous search through antique stores, bathroom showrooms, and eBay.

- **Be mindful of the intended purpose.** Yes, you've fallen in love with that black granite vanity top, but are you going to curse every time someone forgets to wipe it down and you're left with dried water spots? Are your kids going to end up breaking your goose-neck swivel spout faucet because spinning it back and forth is more fun than brushing their teeth? Style is essential, but not at the cost of purpose and functionality.

Lighting

Like my girlfriend says, "There's no such thing as ugly people—only bad lighting." Who wants unflattering lighting, especially when stepping out naked from the shower? So we want lighting that makes us feel good and look good inside the bathroom.

Basically, there are three types of lighting—*overhead*, *accent*, and *task*. With overhead fluorescent lighting being the most unflattering, in every sense, and candle lighting being the most flattering, you have a myriad of options in between.

Overhead

Personally, I can't stand overhead lighting—especially fluorescents. They cast horrific shadows down onto your face that distort your skin tone—never an ego booster. Although traditional fluorescents are greener and more cost efficient than incandescent bulbs, there are a vast array of eco-friendly bulbs such as compact fluorescents (CFLs) and light-emitting diodes (LEDs) that have recently improved their quality of light to be more flattering. Consider some of these more aesthetically pleasing overhead choices for your bathroom:

- **Recessed.** Also referred to as *cans,* these are an ideal choice for medium to large bathrooms. Lights can be strategically placed over places like the shower and toilet and spaced out over the entire room. Remember that if they're installed over a wet area, they must be rated as such. They work very well on dimmers, which allow you to control the amount of light depending on your mood or the time of day.

- **Chandeliers.** Hanging fixtures always offer a sense of drama. Be careful to choose one that will fare well in a damp environment if installing in a full or half bath.

- **Flush mounted.** These are fine for a small bathroom but will not suffice in medium and large ones.

Accent

Accent lighting adds dimension to your bathroom. A spotlight can be use to highlight artwork or a mosaic wall. Two wall sconces can flank your soaking tub. A small shaded lamp can offer warmth and charm when set on an open-faced cabinet shelf. Although intended to complement overhead lighting, accent lights are a must to create a certain look and feel.

Task

No doubt crucial in a bathroom, proper task lighting makes all the difference when it comes to shaving, applying makeup, and tweezing those unsightly hairs. The problem with traditional torchier bar lighting is that it tends to light up the sink but not you. There are those vanity globe bar lights that typically run along the top of the vanity mirror, but though these cast light out (as opposed to down) there's still that problem of casting shadows on your face because they're overhead. A good solution is to install vanity globes that run atop and flank the vanity mirror. This may be too much light all the time, so have them put on a separate switch. Then, when grooming isn't at hand, simply use your overhead recessed light to diffuse light over the entire sink area.

Index

Wiley Publishing, Inc. End-User License Agreement

READ THIS. You should carefully read these terms and conditions before opening the software packet(s) included with this book ("Book"). This is a license agreement "Agreement" between you and Wiley Publishing, Inc. ("WPI"). By opening the accompanying media packet(s), you acknowledge that you have read and accept the following terms and conditions. If you do not agree and do not want to be bound by such terms and conditions, promptly return the Book and the unopened media packet(s) to the place you obtained them for a full refund.

1. **License Grant.** WPI grants to you (either an individual or entity) a nonexclusive license to use one copy of the enclosed media program(s) (collectively, the "Media") solely for your own personal or business purposes on a single computer (whether a standard computer or a workstation component of a multi-user network). The Media is in use on a computer when it is loaded into temporary memory (RAM) or installed into permanent memory (hard disk, CD-ROM, or other storage device). WPI reserves all rights not expressly granted herein.

2. **Ownership.** WPI is the owner of all right, title, and interest, including copyright, in and to the compilation of the Media recorded on the physical packet included with this Book. Copyright to the individual programs recorded on the Media is owned by the author or other authorized copyright owner of each program. Ownership of the Media and all proprietary rights relating thereto remain with WPI and its licensers.

3. **Restrictions on Use and Transfer.**
   (a) You may only (i) make one copy of the Media for backup or archival purposes, or (ii) transfer the Media to a single hard disk, provided that you keep the original for backup or archival purposes. You may not (i) rent or lease the Media, (ii) copy or reproduce the Media through a LAN or other network system or through any computer subscriber system or bulletin-board system, or (iii) modify, adapt, or create derivative works based on the Media.
   (b) You may not reverse engineer, decompile, or disassemble the Media. You may transfer the Media on a permanent basis, provided that the transferee agrees to accept the terms and conditions of this Agreement and you retain no copies. If the Media is an update or has been updated, any transfer must include the most recent update and all prior versions.

4. **Limited Warranty.**
   (a) WPI warrants that the Media are free from defects in materials and workmanship under normal use for a period of sixty (60) days from the date of purchase of this Book. If WPI receives notification within the warranty period of defects in materials or workmanship, WPI will replace the defective Media.
   (b) WPI and the author of the book disclaim all other warranties, express or implied, including without limitation implied warranties of merchantability and fitness for a particular purpose, with respect to the media contained therein, and/or the techniques described in this book. WPI does not warrant that the functions contained in the media will meet your requirements or that the operation of the media will be error free.
   (c) This limited warranty gives you specific legal rights, and you may have other rights that vary from jurisdiction to jurisdiction.

5. **Remedies.**

   (a) WPI's entire liability and your exclusive remedy for defects in materials and workmanship shall be limited to replacement of the Media, which may be returned to WPI with a copy of your receipt at the following address: Software Media Fulfillment Department, Attn.: *Norma Vally's Bathroom Fix-ups*, Wiley Publishing, Inc., 10475 Crosspoint Blvd., Indianapolis, IN 46256, or call (800) 762-2974. Please allow four to six weeks for delivery. This Limited Warranty is void if failure of the Media has resulted from accident, abuse, or misapplication. Any replacement Media will be warranted for the remainder of the original warranty period or thirty (30) days, whichever is longer.

   (b) In no event shall WPI or the author be liable for any damages whatsoever (including without limitation damages for loss of business profits, business interruption, loss of business information, or any other pecuniary loss) arising from the use of or inability to use the Book or the Media, even if WPI has been advised of the possibility of such damages.

   (c) Because some jurisdictions do not allow the exclusion or limitation of liability for consequential or incidental damages, the above limitation or exclusion may not apply to you.

6. **U.S. Government Restricted Rights.** Use, duplication, or disclosure of the Media for or on behalf of the United States of America, its agencies and/or instrumentalities "U.S. Government" is subject to restrictions as stated in paragraph (c)(1)(ii) of the Rights in Technical Data and Computer Software clause of DFARS 252.227-7013, or subparagraphs (c) (1) and (2) of the Commercial Computer Software - Restricted Rights clause at FAR 52.227-19, and in similar clauses in the NASA FAR supplement, as applicable.

7. **General.** This Agreement constitutes the entire understanding of the parties and revokes and supersedes all prior agreements, oral or written, between them and may not be modified or amended except in a writing signed by both parties hereto that specifically refers to this Agreement. This Agreement shall take precedence over any other documents that may be in conflict herewith. If any one or more provisions contained in this Agreement are held by any court or tribunal to be invalid, illegal, or otherwise unenforceable, each and every other provision shall remain in full force and effect.

What's on the DVD?

This appendix provides you with information on the contents of the DVD that accompanies this book.

SYSTEM REQUIREMENTS

If you plan to watch the DVD on your computer, make sure that your computer meets the following minimum system requirements. If your computer doesn't match up to most of these requirements, you may have a problem using the DVD.

- A PC running Windows 98 or later or a Macintosh running Mac OS X
- A DVD-ROM drive

You can also watch the DVD using a regular DVD player.

USING THE DVD

To access the content from the DVD on your computer, follow these steps.

1. Insert the DVD into your computer's DVD-ROM drive. The license agreement appears.

    Note for Windows users: The interface won't launch if you have Autorun disabled. In that case, click Start→Run (For Windows Vista, Start→All Programs→Accessories→Run). In the dialog box that appears, type D:\Start.exe. (Replace D with the proper letter if your DVD drive uses a different letter. If you don't know the letter, see how your DVD drive is listed under My Computer.) Click OK.

    Note for Mac users: The DVD icon will appear on your desktop. Double-click the icon to open the DVD, and then double-click the "Start" icon.

2. Read through the license agreement, and then click the Accept button if you want to use the DVD.

    The DVD interface appears. The interface allows you to play the videos with just a click of a button (or two).

WHAT'S ON THE DVD

On the DVD, you'll find three videos, one from each section of the book. They are:

- Replacing a flush handle
- Replacing a flapper
- Replacing a toilet

TROUBLESHOOTING

If you have difficulty viewing any of the DVD materials on your computer, try the following solutions:

- **Turn off any anti-virus software that you may have running.** Installers sometimes mimic virus activity and can make your computer incorrectly believe that it is being infected by a virus. (Be sure to turn the anti-virus software back on later.)
- **Close all running programs.** The more programs you're running, the less memory is available to other programs. Installers also typically update files and programs; if you keep other programs running, installation may not work properly.

CUSTOMER CARE

If you have trouble with the DVD, please call the Wiley Product Technical Support phone number at (800) 762-2974. Outside the United States, call 1(317) 572-3994. You can also contact Wiley Product Technical Support at **http://support.wiley.com**. John Wiley & Sons will provide technical support only for installation and other general quality control items. For technical support on the applications themselves, consult the program's vendor or author. To place additional orders or to request information about other Wiley products, please call (877) 762-2974.